Teacher's field guide

Teacher's field guide

7 TRUTHS about TEACHING
to
Help You Start Off STRONG,
Avoid Burnout and
Stay in Love with Teaching

kerry hemms
WITH GRAHAM WHITE

NEW YORK

NASHVILLE • MELBOURNE • VANCOUVER

Teacher's field guide
7 TRUTHS about TEACHING to Help You Start Off STRONG, Avoid Burnout, and Stay in Love with Teaching

Published in New York, New York, by Morgan James Publishing. Morgan James is a trademark of Morgan James, LLC. www.MorganJamesPublishing.com

The Morgan James Speakers Group can bring authors to your live event. For more information or to book an event visit The Morgan James Speakers Group at www.TheMorganJamesSpeakersGroup.com.

ISBN 978-1-68350-184-8 paperback
ISBN 978-1-68350-185-5 eBook
ISBN 978-1-68350-186-2 hardcover
Library of Congress Control Number: 2016913584

Cover Design by:
Rachel Lopez
www.r2cdesign.com

In an effort to support local communities, raise awareness and funds, Morgan James Publishing donates a percentage of all book sales for the life of each book to Habitat for Humanity Peninsula and Greater Williamsburg.

Get involved today! Visit
www.MorganJamesBuilds.com

To my late Mommakins, you are missed dearly. Your loving smile still resides deep within my heart. Thank you for your nurturing disposition, which I was able to pass along to my students.

And to Dear Ole Dad, thank you for your constant positive encouragement and for modeling what it means to lead children with the perfect balance of love and firmness.
You are my hero for life.

table of contents

Workload Management 32
Truth #3: You Can Trade Your Bag of Bricks for a Bag of Tips

- How can you lighten your workload so you can breathe?
- How can you simplify things to work smarter, not harder?
- How can you best manage the "other stuff" so you can have a life outside of school?

People Management 47
Truth #4: All Relationships Matter

- How do you successfully manage all of the people and personalities you encounter?
- How do you establish connections with your students when you have so many?
- How do you get along well with administrators, parents, and colleagues, even if you don't see eye to eye with them?

Stress Management 73
Truth #5: There Will Be Days When You Feel Like It's Too Much

- What is the truth about burnout? Why does it happen?
- How can you recognize the symptoms of a teacher on the edge? Is it treatable?
- How do you know if your stress is temporary or if it's really time to quit?

Self-Management 98
Truth #6: Self-Care Is Not Selfish

- How do you successfully take care of yourself as you embrace a life of service?
- How do you nurture your own needs when there are demands that come from all sides?

- How can you give yourself permission to have a healthy work-life balance and realize that self-care is a gift you give your students?

Truth #7: You Will Have Life-Changing Moments That Make It All Worth It

- Is life change really possible?
- How do you keep your focus on the things that really matter when the small stuff is all consuming?
- What is the big picture? Is this really all worth it?

preface

Teachers are heroes.
—**Graham White**

I have always believed that children learn best through modeling. So when I first became a teacher, I made a promise to myself that I would never ask anything of my students that I wasn't modeling for them. If I was going to ask them to be respectful, I would model respect for them at all times. If I expected them to be responsible for their work, then I would be responsible for mine. This was never a problem for me until the one day I realized I was not being true to the promise I made.

I remember the moment I came to that realization. I was teaching my gifted students about the importance of living up to their full potential. I was explaining to them that together we'd work to help them realize their passions, interests, and talents, and then intertwine those qualities in a way that would one day bring purpose to their lives. They could then go on to have great impact and influence in the world. I told them that I wanted them to go *big* and strive to reach their *fullest potential.*

And then I froze. I felt conviction and shame because I wasn't modeling that for them. I knew that there was something big inside of me that needed to come out as well, but I didn't know what it was. I didn't have a mentor leading me through my own process. I knew that I needed to be an example of *finding your big* for my students, but I had no idea how to accomplish this or even where to begin.

I looked for someone who could help me uncover the "big" inside of me and how that might be translated into something meaningful and significant. When I eventually found Graham White (IncrediblePotential.com), I immediately knew he was the one who could help me. But even then, I never imagined our conversations would lead to this book.

Graham led, inspired, and pushed me to share what he described as "an incredibly simple and profoundly impactful approach that is guaranteed to work for students while reducing the stress and workload of the teacher."

His perspective helped me realize how incredibly remarkable, important, and exceptional teachers are. In fact, he was the first person to tell me I was a hero because I was a teacher, and it made me cry. He said that he knows this to be true because his gift is seeing the greatness in people, even when they have yet to recognize it in themselves. He went on to say:

> *"I see every teacher as a hero because the humility necessary to connect heart to heart with children prevents them from boasting about themselves. We accept the idea of a police officer, firefighter, CEO, or general claiming the title of 'Hero,' but teachers are unique in that someone other than them must always acknowledge the title. So I'm saying it: 'Teachers are heroes!'*
>
> *Maybe you can't say it the way I can because you're part of the group that needs to have it claimed by someone else, but you can choose to accept the acknowledgment and be comfortable with*

having it repeated as the chorus and heartbeat of your book—
possibly the only acknowledgment some reading it will ever receive."

With Graham's inspiration, it is my honor to bring you this book. May you also be inspired to reach your full potential and strive to be a remarkable example for those you educate and lead during the course of your career as a teacher. You are a hero!

acknowledgments

I feel humbled and honored to have had so much support in the creation and publication of this book. I never could have done it alone.

It felt a bit like "love at first sight" when I met David Hancock and Bethany Marshall at a publishing event in Atlanta. There was something inside of me that knew this book would find its home within the author-supported framework of Morgan James Publishing.

Terry Whalin, I cannot thank you enough for your patience and encouragement. You took extra time with me, and you made sure I was comfortable and informed in the process. Thank you for always telling me how much you believed in me and in this book. Jim Howard, Margo Toulouse, Nickcole Watkins, and the entire team at Morgan James has treated me like a family member. They are always patient, always prompt in communication, always encouraging, and always ensuring that I am comfortable. I am incredibly honored to partner with you (MorganJamesPublishing.com).

Justin Spizman, your ongoing support and recommendations have made this book a success. Your professional knowledge and expertise were instrumental in architecting a manuscript that exactly expressed the myriad of thoughts and concepts within me, and then you helped me to lay it out in an organized way that the readers could understand. On a personal level, your balance between pushing me and caring for me was exactly what I needed in order to do it. Thank you for being there for me in those delicate moments when I needed you the most, and thank you for handling me and this project with such care and dedication to excellence (JustinSpizman.com).

Thank you to Evie Sacks, who helped polish the manuscript. You have an exquisite eye for detail, and your efforts are much appreciated.

Katherine Rawson, you helped take this manuscript to another level. Thank you so much for your thoughtful suggestions, insights, edits and feedback. This book is better because of you.

Nancy Halseide, your editing and proofreading skills are incredible. I am so grateful for your assistance in making sure all of the intricate details were taken care of.

Dave Ramsey, the decision to follow your advice and wisdom has been life-changing. Thank you for making this entire project possible for this little schoolteacher with big dreams (DaveRamsey.com).

Mr. Brian "Doc" Roberts, you were my first principal and mentor, who went on to be a district executive director. I would not have completed my first year of teaching if it weren't for your support and notes of encouragement along the way. Thank you for giving me the attention that I needed, taking me with you when you opened a new school, and supporting me during my entire teaching career. And here you are 20 years later, still encouraging me through this project and cheerleading my efforts. You are one of kind, Doc! I wish every new teacher could have a principal like you.

Thank you to the faculty and staff at Springfield College in Massachusetts for instilling in me the spirit-mind-body philosophy that helped me bring balance to my teaching life.

Dr. Allison Gilmore, my advisor and associate dean at Mercer University in Atlanta, thank you for preparing me so well for my teaching career. Your program of education is outstanding. You were the first person to tell me I was a strong writer and should write a book. Here it is! Thank you, Dr. Gilmore!

Thank you to the many other people who volunteered their time and insight for this endeavor, including Dr. Gary Childers, Arthur Mills, Kerry Ann Rockquemore, Maria Spagnolo, and the many other teachers and administrators who contributed their thoughts and ideas.

To my "Buckhead Girls," Brooke Mitchell, Catherine Cleary, and Theresa King, you were a dream team to teach with! Thank you for jumping in when I needed you for this project.

Anika White, you have contributed to this project in more ways than you know. Thank you for applying your talents as an artist to the illustrations in this book, and thank you for being so open and helpful in our conversations. You inspired me to ask my students how it felt for them to have their teacher quit in the middle of the year. That offered eye-opening insight. You are a beautiful person, and you are on a wonderful path.

To the students I have taught over the years, you blessed me more than you know. It was my honor to be in your life for the time we had together. A special thank you to my 4th and 5th grade Talented and Gifted (TAG) students who contributed their ideas and thoughts to this project. I wanted to be sure that student voices were heard, and you were beautifully willing to share.

I have been fortunate to experience many different school environments over the years, all of which gave me a better understanding of my teaching practice as I tried to figure out what works and what doesn't. Thank you to all of the school districts who were part of my journey through teaching.

To my husband, Ray, you are my rock and lovebug all in one. Your patience and commitment to helping this book come to fruition is beyond words. Thank you for being by my side the entire way, sprinkling me with some lighthearted humor when I needed it, and for not letting me give up when I wanted to.

And to my *incredible family*, thank you for your ongoing love and support in my life and in this process. Our closeness, friendship, and abiding unconditional love are blessings for which I am grateful every single day.

introduction

Dear Journal,

I have just been hired for my first teaching job! I can't wait! I have so many ideas! Hurry up time; hurry up! When is summer going to end? When can I move in to set up my classroom? When? I can't wait!

Kerry

.... ✿ ....

Dear Journal,

It is one month into the school year. I don't have time to write because I'm too overwhelmed. NEED SLEEP.

Kerry

.... ✿ ....

Dear Journal,

It is now November break in my first year of teaching. I'm not sure I'm going to make it. I cry in the mornings on my way to school because it is so hard and I am so tired. I am up late every night working on lesson plans or grading. Yesterday, one of my students was banging his head against a brick wall, over and over, and crying. He refused to walk down the hall with us for art class, and just kept banging. When I asked him what was going on, he said that his mom said he was useless because he forgot to iron his jeans. What do I do with that? I had no idea it would be like this! Is this what "teaching" is like? What did I just sign up for? Please help.

Kerry

.... ✿ ....

While writing these journal entries 20 years ago, I wondered if I was alone. Was I the only one to ever feel this way? Over the years, as I watched teacher after teacher leave the profession too soon, I have realized the answer to that question. I have found out that most teachers feel exactly the same way that I did when I first started teaching, but everyone is too ashamed to tell anyone else. They think that if they admit they are struggling, it would be a sign of weakness and incompetence. Unfortunately, this silent suffering has led us to the very real problem facing the teaching profession today.

The Problem

Did you know that *10 percent* of new teachers do not make it through their first year, and that November is the most common quitting time? Are you aware that within their first five years, *50 percent* of new teachers leave the profession?

I am saddened watching new teachers drop out all around me, and I believe my fellow teachers would be in agreement that it's worse now than ever before. Even some veteran teachers are quitting before the year is over. A couple of years ago, an experienced teacher two doors down from me quit with only one month to go in the school year. Last year, I watched one classroom turn over three different teachers! Not to mention all of the substitute teachers in between.

Retaining teachers is getting harder and harder. One nearby school is losing 14 teachers at the end of this year, and those are just the ones giving advanced notice.

Sadly, this is happening everywhere. It is not uncommon. It is not regional. It is not even just our nation.

In the UK, teaching is recognized as one of the most stressful occupations, with rates of suicide running at a third above the national average.[1] In fact, in the UK, *40 percent* of teachers quit in their first year.[2] In Canada, constant stress, overwork, and emotional exhaustion suffocate the profession, and the overall health of teachers suffers dearly.[3] In Australia, an Australian Education Union report reveals that stressed teachers are quitting over high workloads.[4]

In addition to the retention problem costing our nation *billions* (if I told you the number your jaw would drop), perhaps even more concerning is that enrollment in teacher preparation programs is falling at alarming rates.

Recently, a survey of 53,000 teachers was conducted asking for input on why so many are leaving and if they would encourage their students or loved ones to become teachers. *Two-thirds* of the 53,000 teachers surveyed would *not* recommend teaching as a profession![5]

We cannot allow this to continue. We need a solution to the crisis in the teaching profession, and that is the purpose of this book.

---

1   http://www.theguardian.com/education/2013/may/01/headteacher-kills-herself
2   http://www.dailymail.co.uk/news/article-3020255/Four-10-new-teachers-don-t-YEAR-classroom-exhausted-stressed-colleagues-says-union-boss.html
3   http://www.cbc.ca/news/canada/teacher-stress-is-killing-my-profession-1.789436
4   http://www.news.com.au/national/stressed-teachers-quitting-over-high-workload-australian-education-union-report-reveals/story-fncynjr2-1227349535411
5   https://www.gadoe.org/External-Affairs-and-Policy/communications/Documents/Teacher%20Survey%20Results.pdf

A Solution with Results

I wrote *Teacher's Field Guide* to make sure you do not become part of the crisis. Together, we are going to walk through *7 Truths about Teaching*, and in doing so you will learn everything you need to know about how to love your life as a teacher, even when it gets hard.

As you can see from my journal entries above, there have been many times that I struggled. I often wondered if there was something wrong with me because I didn't love my life as a teacher. I was too embarrassed and ashamed to admit that I was in over my head and wanted to quit. It was never the kids—it was always the "other stuff." Although I loved the act and art of teaching, I just didn't love *my life* as a teacher. I felt like I had no life, actually. It was all-consuming. All of the demands, paperwork, and pressure completely wore me out.

I remember coming home and collapsing out of exhaustion. Sometimes I would cry on my pillow out of helplessness. I remember blaming myself and thinking that I must not be cut out for this, because everyone else seemed fine. I would constantly question if I made the right choice in choosing to teach, and I wondered if my students could see my inner turmoil.

I even know what it's like to be at the end of the line and not be able to make it through the school year. Yes, I was part of that five-year statistic. I regrettably did not make it through my fifth year and had to leave my students.

But thankfully, I returned the next year. And when I did, everything changed. Before our time together is finished, you will read about my life-changing moment that was the catalyst for an incredible shift in perspective. Through that experience, I decided to learn from my mistakes, master a new way of thinking, clarify my systems, and implement strategies that have lasting value.

Now, I am honored to say that I have been a teacher for 20 wonderful years. I have taught in 3 regions of the country, set up 15 classrooms, and have worked in 8 different schools ranging from Title I to prestigious. I cannot wait to share with you the systems and strategies I learned along the way. My hope is that you will be spared feelings of desperation and isolation that so many before you have endured.

The strategies and systems you will read about are the reasons I fell back in love with teaching. I learned to not only love the art of teaching but to love *my life* as a teacher as well.

I never would have imagined this new approach could result in hundreds of positive notes from students, parents, and administrators. These are comments that I keep in a special box (I call it my "Love Note Box") that I will never forget. These notes inspired me to forge forward to create this book in the hopes that it could make a difference in the lives of students through caring teachers like you.

It is with gratitude and humility that I offer you a peek into that very special box:

From Students

"You believe in me, even though my life is hard."

"Thank you so much. You helped me figure out who I am, and I'm only 10."

"I am grateful to have you be one of the people that I know in my life."

"You will always be the teacher that I remember. Thank you for caring about me."

"You taught me to never give up, even when life and school gets rough. I can't thank you enough."

"Thank you for what you did for me and us. You keep me safe."

"I appreciate you because you are always calm and you never yell."

"I want to be a teacher someday—just like you!"

From Parents

"Every parent hopes and prays for a teacher like you."

"My child loves school now, and it's all because of you."

"Thanks for showing these children that you could teach them and love them all at the same time."

"You were the perfect balance of love and firmness for my son."

"All I can say is thank you. I can't find the words for our appreciation and gratitude. You were instrumental in my daughter's life. Thank you for loving her."

"You have worked a miracle in my child."

From Administrators

"You are one of the most talented teachers I've had the privilege of working with."

"You individualize learning for all students."

"You have created a student-centered classroom where students feel valued and trust you."

"Excellent classroom management skills."

"You are the most positive staff member we have."

"You are very calm, consistent, and caring. You are doing a great job with your students."

"You have created a warm, engaging learning environment. You model caring, respect, and enthusiasm for learning."

"Your students couldn't help but love being in your class! They know you believe in them."

"Thank you for being a ray of sunshine in our school by always smiling and encouraging others."

From the State of Georgia: A RESOLUTION

"WHEREAS, a proper quality education for the young people of this state is the single most important objective of the General

Assembly ... as a result of appreciable gains in student achievement and dedication to students and the profession ... it is abundantly fitting and proper that outstanding contributions to the education and welfare of young people be recognized ... BE IT RESOLVED that Kerry J. Venuti [Hemms] is commended for tireless efforts on behalf of public education, congratulated, and extended most sincere best wishes for future success."

From the United States Senate in Washington, D.C.

"It is a pleasure to send my heartfelt congratulations to you upon earning the Master Teacher Certification. By receiving this recognition, you have demonstrated your outstanding ability to inspire students ... You love the classroom and know that the bright and eager young minds you see each day depend on you for guidance ... You are a perfect example of what a teacher should be."

Teachers, Please Know ...

I do not share these comments with you to brag. I only share them with you so you will know what is possible for you when you apply the techniques in this book. Those comments or recognitions did not come by overworking myself or by putting in too many long hours. In fact, with my renewed approach, I was never known to stay extra late after school, volunteer incessantly, or obsess on the weekends about school. Actually, it was quite the opposite. These results came as a side effect of my new way of thinking, which you will learn about in this book. After I changed the way I approached my life as a teacher, my joy returned, and that impacted everything. I wasn't ever trying to gain any recognition; it just happened.

While I am honored and humbled to receive them, status and awards are not what motivate me. What matters to me are the students. *Am I making a difference? Am I doing my best while maintaining a healthy balance in my life? Am I showing up with enough to give? Will anyone be changed because they knew me?* These are the questions that drive me. I look forward to sharing with you the exact blueprint to put in place that will help you get the same results.

Welcome to a New Approach

I am thrilled you are reading this book. Welcome to starting off strong if you are new, or welcome to a new beginning, a new approach, and a new perspective if you are an experienced teacher. I cannot wait to reveal to you the things I have figured out that make teaching a joy and an honor, while not allowing "the other stuff" to ruin it.

The book is designed for easy navigation. You can read it straight through, or you can jump around. It is divided into seven sections, or *7 Truths*. Each Truth (T) is a pillar in your life as a teacher, and together, the seven pillars support an organizational framework of *management*:

- T1—Mindset Management
- T2—Classroom Management
- T3—Workload Management
- T4—People Management
- T5—Stress Management
- T6—Self-Management
- T7—Big Picture Management

As you journey through this book, you will discover answers to many questions, including the following:

- Why did I choose teaching, and what will my end story be?
- How can I really make a difference when it's so stressful?
- What is the simplest and easiest classroom management plan that really works?

- How do I have a life outside of school when the workload never ends?
- What is the secret to having great relationships with students, parents, administrators, and colleagues?
- What's the deal with burnout? How do I know if I have it, and what should I do if it's there?
- How do I take care of myself when I'm taking care of others all of the time?
- How can I find support when no one will help me or when I'm afraid to ask?
- Is this really all worth it?

I think you are going to be pleasantly surprised to learn that yes, you can do this. You *can* have a life you love *and* make a difference in the lives of so many. I want you to embrace your life in this profession and feel proud to call yourself a teacher.

That reminds me of one last thing before we dive in. Let's make sure we are all on the same page...

What Is a Teacher?

Tell someone you're a soldier or a firefighter and you'll have his or her respect and admiration. Mention that you're a doctor or a lawyer and you'll have instant status. But tell people you're a teacher and what's their reaction? Is it positive, or hesitant? Has the perception of teaching been influenced negatively by the teacher bashing we all hear about?

It's true that we desperately need stories that will help strengthen and encourage teachers, but if you're waiting for that to happen, you will miss it. It is not up to the press or anyone else to encourage us. We need to dig deep inside of ourselves and believe that we matter. Some people may never get it, and that's okay. What matters is that *we* get it.

Choosing to be a teacher is a statement of service and sacrifice. It's knowingly taking a path that will demand your heart as well as your soul. Being a teacher is a gift that you willingly give every day to a room full of individuals who can't understand or appreciate the loving sacrifice you make when you walk through those doors.

You might not feel like it yet, but the truth is that as a teacher, you have an opportunity every day to be a hero. It's easy to take for granted that you have such a powerful position in students' lives. But if you take enough care of yourself so you can be aware of what's really happening in the lives of your students, there will be times when a few words from you can brighten their day and possibly even change the entire trajectory of their lives. This unequivocally makes you a living, breathing, life-changing hero. So there you have it! If you've never heard it before, here is the truth about teachers: They are heroes. And that means you, but don't take my word for it.

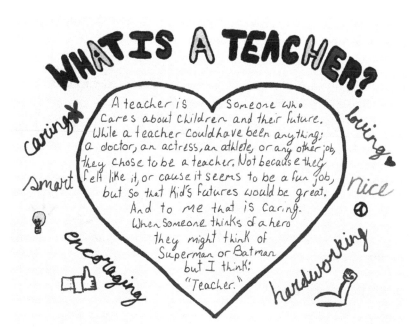

Recently, with absolutely no guidance or direction, I asked my students to respond to the question "What is a teacher?" in any way they wanted. Some wrote letters, some drew pictures, and while all of them were quite moving in their own way, I believe that one says it all.

My Promise and Hope

As we embark upon this wonderful journey together, I hope that you find everything you need to love your life as a teacher. If I missed anything, or if you want to dive deeper, I promise to let you know how to communicate with me at the end of this book.

As you read *Teacher's Field Guide*, my hope is that you hold tightly to three things:

1. **You are a hero.** You matter. Your decision to join this profession of heart-centered individuals makes you extraordinary.
2. **Your joy in this profession matters.** You deserve to love your life as a teacher. You deserve to have the tools and strategies you need to make an impact without losing your life and mind in the process.
3. **You are not alone.** This profession is HARD. I know it, and you know it. No one understands what it's like to walk in the shoes of a teacher unless they have done it themselves. I get it, and I am committed to making sure you feel supported and encouraged in the process.

So, let's get going!

To all of the highly devoted new and experienced teachers out there, may you be strengthened, may you be encouraged, and may you love your life as a teacher.

Let the journey begin!

mindset management

Truth #1: We Begin with a Vision

Where there is no vision, there is no hope.
—George Washington Carver

Make Sure You Have Your Teaching Bookends in Place

I f you are a new teacher, welcome to the most exciting journey of your life! I am so excited for you. If you are an experienced teacher, welcome to a fresh, new beginning! I know you are busy and your time is valuable, so we are going to get going right away by putting your "teaching bookends" into place. I believe that these will create the foundation for everything to come and will give you the biggest advantage possible for a long, successful teaching career.

The first bookend has to do with thinking about *why* we decided to become teachers in the first place. This is not a profession that we chose because we heard whispers about enormous salaries or fabulous vacation packages. We chose this profession because there is something in our hearts that wants to make a difference in the lives of others—specifically in the lives of children.

This makes teaching one of the most noble and heroic professions. It is the product of a higher calling, a soulful feeling, and a burning desire to impact future generations. As teachers, we make the conscious decision to join the greater good and leave our mark on young men and women in the classroom.

Which leads us to the other bookend: *our legacy*.

Over the course of your career, you will police the halls, break up arguments, and solve the mysteries of missing clothes, lunches, and homework. There will be many eyes to dry and quivering lips to still. You will ease the concern of parents who find it hard to accept the responsibility their child had in a situation, and you will nurse a wide assortment of sore stomachs, scrapes, bumps, and bruises. You will listen to heartbreaking stories, soothe hurt feelings, and help hundreds develop a better understanding of themselves and life.

In short, you will make a difference. You will leave a legacy that the little lives you touch will remember because teachers change lives—*lots* of lives. We do so every minute, every hour, every day, every week, and every school year. This happens because *we care*. We know that each student is valuable and beautiful in his or her own unique way. We care about the boys, about the girls, about their development, and about their education. That caring changes lives and leaves a legacy.

So, let's get busy setting up your bookshelf! Are you ready? You are now going to put the first bookend in place, which is the reason you decided to become a teacher.

The First Bookend: Your Why

When people used to ask me why I became a teacher, I would be at a loss for words. I would freeze, maybe as a defense mechanism, to block criticism and to protect myself. I would almost always want to say: "Why are you asking why? Are you inquiring because you are truly curious? Or are you asking it as in *out of everything possible, why reduce yourself to teaching?*"

As I reflect on the question today, I think people ask because they're in awe of the enormous responsibility we undertake. They look at the challenge of managing their own children and wonder, "Who would intentionally sign up to take on 25 or more of these creatures that they haven't even given birth to?!" They're wondering how we have the size of heart and the amount of energy it takes to be able to love and lead so many, including their own, day after day, year after year. It may not be the words that cross their lips, but they're looking at us and wondering if who they see is a hero.

Our reasons for teaching are seldom as simple as a one-sentence answer, and our reasons may change over the years. But these are the most common answers I've heard when teachers are asked why they chose teaching:

- "I wanted to do something where I felt I could make a difference."
- "I love working with children/young people."
- "I wanted a job that felt challenging, and I knew no two days would be the same."
- "I had a teacher who showed me I mattered, that I was special, and that I was great at something. It inspired me to want to be able to do the same."
- "I'm passionate about (my subject)! I loved the idea that I could share what I think is amazing with others. I can't imagine anything better than seeing someone light up when this makes sense and then watching as it becomes a passion for them!"

My personal path to teaching began at the age of 12. I was an active gymnast, practicing for three to four hours per day, four days per week. After school, I would walk to the gym, show up early to practice, and I would sit on the floor doing my homework while other classes were in progress. I started to occasionally engage with the younger students who were having classes before me, and my coach noticed.

She surprised me when she asked me to teach some classes, starting with a "Mom and Tot" class. *What? Me?* I was intimidated and thought it was a joke. *Why me?* I wondered. *I am only a tween!* I decided to give it a try, and it was such a natural connection for me that I ended up teaching classes of all levels until I graduated high school. There was something that felt dutiful and lovely about instructing the young gymnasts, and this would become a feeling that would never leave me. It was through this experience that helping others learn became my life's purpose.

When I was a senior, I taught the daughter of Mr. Holbrook, my high school homeroom and physics teacher. Talk about awkward. He would watch me teach the class, and I always secretly wondered, "Is he grading me?" I could only begin to consider what would happen if his child didn't excel. It was weird! Although I was tempted to put on an impressive dog and pony show, I held back the urge to do anything different or overly spectacular when he watched. I learned to ignore the pressure and just go for it. In doing so, I ended up enjoying his cute little daughter just as much as the others. But I never knew what he thought of me.

The summer after my high school graduation, my dad unexpectedly ran into Mr. Holbrook at one of our small town events. When my father came home, I wasn't sure what to think because he was slightly choked up while telling me about his run-in. I thought for sure that I blew it! I got nervous over the thought of letting him down. He went on to explain that Mr. Holbrook had approached him, shook his hand, looked him in the eye, and said, "I hope my daughter grows up to be just like yours." I gulped. We then enjoyed a long hug, and both of us wallowed in that special moment of gratitude.

The reason those words carried such profound meaning is because my dad raised me on his own. My parents divorced when I turned six, and my father had full custody of all four children. He parented alone and felt solely responsible for the way I turned out as a high school senior. But I wasn't the result of a single parent as much as I was the result of a single parent who understood the value of loving us to the core and making sure we were under the influence of good teachers.

When school began the fall after my parents' divorce, I remember feeling unstable because I was starting my first day of first grade without a mom. I was mad! And sad! And really confused. Although I made myself look fine for the daytime hours, I constantly cried myself to sleep at night, unable to comprehend it all. It felt like my world was tumbling down around me.

So as I started school, I came to some very difficult realizations. I learned that I didn't fit in. I learned that something was different about me. I learned that I was the only one I knew who couldn't start or finish any sentences with the words "my mom."

Despite his unconditional love and guidance, my dad couldn't help me at school as I was sitting at my desk feeling so confused and surrounded with loss. I missed my mom every single day. I couldn't make sense of it. Why would I be the one without the welcome home kiss? Without soft hands going through my hair, giving me a hug, and asking questions about my day? Why everyone else, but not me?

And yet, in the midst of it all, something wonderful happened. And it happened not only that year, but also the year after that, the year after that, and the year after that. I learned my most valuable lesson: the power of a teacher. Every year I was matched with a new hero who gave me just the right amount of love and nurturing that I needed. They looked after me and even let me hold their hands. I remember the joy in that sensation like it was yesterday.

One day, I remember asking my first grade teacher if I could brush her beautiful long hair instead of playing outside for recess. She said yes because she knew my unique situation, and what I really needed at that time. She knew what many of us know: love and acceptance are two of our most basic needs, and she gifted me with just that. It was a connection I was craving, and she sacrificed for me. It wasn't just her but all the teachers that followed. My teachers gave me the love and acceptance that I needed to grow into a healthy, strong woman.

That was their gift. While I may not have had a mom to go home to after school, all of my elementary school teachers made me feel like I had a mom between the hours of 7 a.m. to 3 p.m. every day. It wasn't everyone's normal, but it was *my* normal, and I learned to love it. I was going to be okay after all! That is the power of teachers. And that is what inspired me to become one myself so I could pass along the nurturing my teachers gave me.

So, there you have it. That is why I teach—not exactly a one-sentence answer! And while I can only imagine that many of my teachers did not intend to play mother and nurture a young kid searching to fill a void, they generously did it. Not necessarily because they set out to do so, but because opportunity called and they stepped up. That is the beauty of teaching.

As teachers, we have the opportunity to be so much to so many.

Now that I have shared my bookend of why I decided to become a teacher, I want you to take some time to reflect on your own. Why did you choose teaching? What is your story? When things get hard, you'll want a reminder of why you decided to become a teacher in the first place. Because on the toughest of days, underneath all of the stress, your reason, motivation, and inspiration will still be there. No one can take that away. You are important, and the path that led you to join this beautiful profession of heroes is worthy of expression.

Close your eyes and think back to the beginning. Think back to before the stained shirts, the boxed lunches, and the busy hallways. Then answer the important question: Why did you choose to teach? Write your answer below.

_____

_____

_____

_____

_____

_____

I hope you found value in this exercise. Hold on tight to your *why*.

While it is of utmost importance to recall our beginnings, we also need to envision our ending and set intentions for the impact we hope to have. Everything in between is the beautiful journey called teaching. With the bookend of why you began in the first place, let's look at the other piece: your legacy.

The Second Bookend: Your Legacy

> *Begin with the end in mind.*
> —Steven Covey

Would you find it inspiring, intimidating, or unbelievable if I told you that the potential you possess as a teacher with passion and heart is the most powerful force for change on the planet today? As teachers, we are gifted with an enormous responsibility, one that is extremely important and vital to the development of future generations: We are given the task of shaping lives. By remembering to do the work while keeping the end in mind, we can know that the value of what we do is more than making it to the end of the day or the end of the year.

If you teach elementary school, you will see an average of 25 or more new students each year. If you are in secondary education, you will likely meet hundreds. Consider what that amounts to over the average career of a teacher. Think about all of these students gathered in one place on your last day of teaching. On that day of retirement, many years from now…

- What is it you hope your students will say?
- What is the legacy that you hope to leave with them?
- What difference will you have made in their lives?

If we set the intention from the start, we can leave a substantial and lasting mark on the students who come through our classroom door. It may not feel like a lot in the context of a single year, but over the course of a career, we can impact hundreds, even thousands, of students: the way they feel about themselves, their potential, and their contribution to the world. Few jobs offer so much opportunity to affect so many lives, and that's what makes this a profession filled with heroes.

If imagining your legacy is hard for you to do, try thinking about your own personal experience. If I asked you to name your favorite teacher, who would come to mind? Why? Maybe it was someone who believed in you when no one else did, made you feel like you mattered, or who refused to allow you to settle for less than they knew you could achieve. Did anyone influence you? What were the qualities of that individual who made you want to believe in yourself, to reach higher and to work harder than anyone else? What is it that made them shine?

After you finish answering those questions, think about what impact you want to make on your students. If they were asked the same questions, what are the words that you would hope they would use in describing you? What kind of teacher do you want to be remembered as?

This is your future legacy:

_____

_____

_____

_____

_____

_____

_____

It takes courage to think through these questions. I know it is not easy to think about the end, especially when you are excited to get started! But it is important.

As you journey through the bookends of teaching, always remember that it takes just one great teacher to change a life, and you can be that one. Remember why you started, and clearly envision your legacy.

Now that we have our two solid bookends in place, let's begin setting you up to write many "books" to fill your shelf. Each year a new book will be added to your personal teaching bookshelf: Year One, Year Two ... just like a playlist. There will be up years, and there will be down years. But the beauty is within the pages. Let's make sure that your pages are filled with wonderful moments that make you proud to be a teacher. We will start with making sure you are creating the best environment possible for you and your students to thrive, making your legacy come to life.

classroom management

Truth #2: If You Don't Have a Plan Before the Students Arrive, They Will Eat You Alive

By failing to prepare, you are preparing to fail.
—Benjamin Franklin

I'm sure in your teacher training, everyone told you about the importance of classroom management. If you are an experienced teacher, you know they were right. It is the single most important structure to have in place, but a lot of teachers make it harder than it needs to be. There is a simple and effective way to run a classroom, and I'm going to share the strategies and tips that have worked for me time and time again, regardless of the type of classroom or educational environment.

Classroom Management Made Easy

Imagine a classroom where every student feels safe, loved, challenged, and understood. Imagine an environment for learning that makes visitors feel welcomed and comfortable. Imagine you, the teacher, being able to trust your students to make the right choices while you are engaged in relevant personalized lessons. Imagine your classroom being a place where students love to be and where they hate to leave.

You may not be able to control what content standards you are required to teach or what initiatives you must follow, but you have full control over the learning environment. Before any teaching takes place, the environment must be set up for learning.

Most teachers do the opposite. They think they must master lesson content and teaching methodologies, but they neglect to prepare for how to manage the environment for learning. They spend hours and hours on lesson plans and unit plans, and then they realize when they go to teach that they are wasting valuable time on managing behaviors. They spend the entire year feeling constantly frustrated and falling behind in the curriculum because so much time is wasted. I am advising you to spend your front-end time on the *environment*, and *then* plan and deliver lessons.

Environment first, teaching second.

When it comes to the learning environment, the teacher is the creator. It is up to *you* to create an environment for learning that both you and your students absolutely love. But it doesn't happen by accident, chance, or luck. It happens because you take the time and energy to envision, plan, commit, and then execute. And all of this begins well before the first day.

As a teacher, you already know that the majority of your work occurs outside of the classroom—this is especially true when planning for the first day of class. It can be overwhelming, even for the most seasoned of teachers, which is why I have put together a planning guide to make sure your first day sets you up for a year of success. We are going to walk through the very same planning that I go through each year. This process has worked well for me over the years. You may choose to model it or just use it to initiate brainstorming for your own style. There are many, many ways to set up successful classrooms, but this is what has worked for me.

Before the First Day

Every new school year brings new opportunity. Whether it is your first year or your twentieth, the days leading up to the start of school are of the utmost importance. Think of your summer as one big planning period. It is your chance to decompress and plan the year ahead. But let's remember, I'm not talking about lesson plans; I'm talking about an environment plan. Or, what I like to call *a business plan*. Yes, you read that right.

My best recommendation is to set your classroom up to run like a mini-business. I have continually done this and I believe it is the reason my classroom ends up running itself, even when there's a sub. The secret is that by automating the "business," the teacher is freed up to work on other things like lesson planning and pedagogy. It also frees the teacher up to give individual attention to students, as needed.

Don't worry. You can do this! Once you get the hang of the setup, it will become easy to implement, and I am confident that you'll never look back.

Here is my process. Follow these steps, and you will create a classroom that functions like a dream.

Step 1: Envision

This first step begins in the mind, and it can even be done poolside. Clearly envision your version of ideal. This is your time to dream up what may seem impossible but is actually achievable. Use your imagination to design and create your ideal classroom.

- What does your perfectly run classroom look like? Feel like? Sound like?
- How are the students interacting with one another?
- What kind of movement is in the room?
- What is the tone?

For example, I prefer a peaceful, soft environment. That is how I work best. Notice I said "I" and not "students." This is because my classroom has to be right for who I am and how I will achieve my personal best. The environment I live in (my classroom) has to match. If I couldn't tolerate a lot of noise, why in the world would I create a loud environment? This would only work to unsettle my focus and negatively affect my composure. By ensuring the environment is best suited for *my* maximum performance, I ensure that my students receive my absolute best.

This isn't selfish. It is being aware of how you can best serve your students. Remember, the teacher is the creator of the classroom environment. Some teachers get annoyed by the chaos and think that the students can't stop chatting. They are wrong. They can, but they need a leader with vision and commitment.

If you never envision your ideal, then your ideal can never happen.

To the new teachers: When you master this step, you will find yourself ahead of most veteran peers. Take the time to visualize your ideal atmosphere. You will be glad you did.

Step 2: Planning

This step requires writing, so make sure you have what you need. You are going to make two correlating lists in the form of a T chart (or whatever makes sense for you). One side should be labeled "task" and the other labeled "procedure."

You are going to brainstorm every single possible routine and nonroutine task that ultimately becomes part of your students' day, and then you will outline the procedure for that task. So, for this exercise, you are entering the mind of your students. Think about what they will be wondering when they are in your classroom.

I truly believe that students want to do the right thing. They just need to know what the right thing is! For example, have you ever traveled to a foreign country? Or joined a club? Or tried to play a new sport? When we first enter an unfamiliar place, we quickly try to figure out how everything works. We want to know what we are supposed to be doing. This is exactly what your students want to know—they are new to your classroom and want to find their place. The good news is that you are going to make it easy for them by taking the time to plan.

What are the everyday things that come up in any given school day? For example, a student enters your room, and he or she immediately thinks, where do I go? What do I do? Knowing this, the very first time I meet the students, I explain to them where they go and what they do. We do this each and every day. It is called a routine task. It is predictable and comfortable. And the students like it.

When you explain *how* to proceed through a certain routine task, it is called a procedure. If you would like to set up your classroom to run in a comfortable and flawless way, you need to put clear routines and procedures in place. For example, do you wonder why your noisy pencil sharpener is running all day at the worst times? It is because there is not a procedure in place for the routine task of pencil sharpening. In my classroom, the procedure is that pencil sharpening is done only in the last 10 minutes of the day. That's it. I do not allow it first thing in the morning or during the day because I (and others) can't stand the noise. If they have a pencil issue during the instructional day, they will use their problem-solving skills (which we talk about regularly) to solve it.

Be patient with this step. Brainstorming every routine task that occurs during the course of a day in your classroom (restrooms, drinks, snacks, handing in papers, notes for the teacher, asking for help, homework, managing papers, managing devices and books, lining up, end of day, etc.) takes considerable time. You may want to start with the list of tasks first, and then think about the procedure for each one.

A valuable time saver is to focus extra attention on transition procedures. It helps the students' productivity level when procedures are in place for how to transition around the room (for example, from desks to carpet area) or for lining up, and even for how to transition from one subject to the next. The goal is to optimize instructional time. I always think, what is the fastest, most efficient way to transition? How can this be done quickly and quietly? For upper grades, think about their routine for entering your room. Consider what they will do as soon as they enter that will set the tone for learning, not socializing. For elementary teachers, this concept also applies to walking in the hallways. With my students, we practice going from point A to point B in one straight and quiet line. Not because I want to "control" them, but because it is the most efficient, respectful, and acceptable way to travel through the hallways in a school where learning is taking place, and I am responsible for their safety. This is just one example; rest assured you will find the things that matter the most to you.

Remember, every listed item gets a clear procedure that makes sense to you and will be understandable for the students. As you make your lists, ask yourself, is this bringing me closer to successfully creating the vision I had in Step 1? Be sure everything aligns with the environment you wish to create. Keep it simple but clear, and be sure you can commit to teaching them the procedures for tasks just like you would teach any lesson. Don't just tell them without modeling and rehearsing. Provide them with practice time to demonstrate mastery of the expectations, and give positive reinforcement when the procedures are practiced appropriately. Consistency will be your friend.

For those who love planning and want to take it a step further, make a *Classroom Procedures/Policies Manual*. This is time-consuming, but the summer is the perfect time to do it. Additionally, it might be something that you could actually hand out to the students and even parents. I have never done this, but I can see the benefit of it if you are driven to do so.

Step 3: Physical Environment

This step addresses the process of setting up the physical environment. It may not be possible until you actually get into your classroom to see what you are working with; however, there are a few things that will be the same no matter the situation. Most importantly, you want the physical environment to coincide with your vision. There is no right or wrong way to set up your room, and it can change throughout the year.

To begin, you'll need to clearly envision the flow of the day, how you and your students need to move, and the required materials. Then, you will set up your classroom in a way that facilitates your vision. I always do a floor plan on paper first, and I think about it in terms of flow (ease of movement) and zones. For help with this plan, I ask myself these guiding questions:

- Where do I want to position my desk and my personal supplies in the room? (Teacher Zone)
- Where should I place all of the student-only supplies? (Student Zone)

- Where will the computers and other technology-related items go? (Tech Zone)
- Where will we gather as a community? (Class Meeting Zone)

You get the idea. For me, it helps to think about things in terms of groupings, meaning identifying things that go together. For example, it does not make sense for my students to have to go one place to get notebook paper and across the room for scissors. I put it all in the same area.

Notice I haven't mentioned desks yet. Whenever I am setting up a new classroom (I have set up 15 and counting), the first thing I do is shove all of the desks together in the middle front of the room, which makes a giant table. I know that this is generally where they will be sitting, so it doesn't matter at this point how I group them. That is done last. Instead, that giant table becomes my organizing place for posters, boxes, etc. while I set up the rest of my room. The very last thing I do is arrange the desks.

When you are ready to think about it, the desk arrangement should align with the learning environment you seek to create. For example, if you are envisioning a lot of team or group learning, you are not going to put your desks in separated rows. Rather, you would put them in tables of four or pairs of two. Conversely, if your students will work best in a more traditional formation, choose one that keeps their attention forward. Whatever you choose, my advice would be to make sure that the students are situated in a way that minimizes distractions and maximizes focus. Middle and high school teachers may not have a choice in this area, so only seek to manage the things you actually can control.

As for the rest of the furniture and storage spaces in the room, I (again) think about flow. How will we be moving around this room, and where is the logical place to put those materials? It requires a lot of planning, and sometimes I will use sticky notes and put them up around the room as I try to figure it out. I do this for the bookshelves as well. I ask myself questions like: What makes the most sense to go there? What needs easy access, and what is barely ever used? All of these details matter. My room setup is of paramount importance to me because I am someone who doesn't do well in chaos. For me to be my best, I need organization and neatness. It takes me a long time to set up my rooms, but it's always worth it. If you can get into school early to do this, I highly recommend it.

Lastly, don't forget to think about other things like lighting (lamps are fantastic), special seating, what students see on the wall, accessories like plants, and whether or not you will play classical music or other sounds to create atmosphere. I always think of my classroom like a little apartment. The goal is to set up an environment that you absolutely love being in. In doing so, your students will love being there too.

Step 4: Start with a Great First Day

In this last step, you will write down your lesson plan for the first day of school, which will include going over the relevant procedures and expectations *for that day only*. You don't want to bombard the students with every single procedure, but you will need to address all of the ones they need for success on that day.

For example, five minutes before lunch I say, "Okay class, it is almost lunch time. Here is how it works. First, you will …" Then, before reentering the room after lunch, I stop them at the door and say, "Class, this is how we enter the room after lunch. First, we …" The idea is to help them be successful. At the end of the day, you want them to leave your class thinking, "Yes! I can do this! I can and will be successful in this room. I know what to do, and therefore I feel safe."

As for your other plans, the first day of school can be approached in many different ways. Initially, I thought it was supposed to be a get-to-know-you day, filled with lots of games and activities. I quickly learned that was a bad idea for me. It taught the students that this room was going to be fun and loose, almost like an indoor recess. That is *not* the message I want to give on the first day. So now I set it up for business and appropriate schoolwork. My first day is just like the days that follow, except that procedures have to be explained and practiced. That makes it less confusing for the students and gets them right to work.

If you choose to adopt this mindset, you'll be setting the room up for learning, not playing. Isn't that why they are there? By establishing a working environment even on the first day, you are communicating a lot of things. You are showing them the expectation without telling them. You are letting them experience right off the bat what it's like to be in your organized and caring classroom, which makes them feel safe. In this way, they are being trained for success, not failure.

If you are a new teacher, this may be confusing and overwhelming. I get it! For those who might be interested, the following is an example of what your first day might look like if you are an elementary school teacher. Middle and high school teachers, I would imagine that your day would be a shorter and matured version of this, and that you would repeat it several times throughout the course of that first day. (Note: This is the framework that I've found works for me time and time again, but that doesn't mean there's no other way. Every teacher is different, and you will find your own style.)

The First Day Example

Arrival

- Many elementary students will be accompanied by their parents on the first day. You've planned well, so there's nothing left to do but smile and greet. Treat them and their parents like royalty (see Truth #4 about first impressions).

- The students will arrive with supplies in hand. They will wonder where to go and what to do, which means it is time to implement your plan.

- There is a very clear and guaranteed-to-be-understood task on their desk. In addition to that, write the directions on the board for a visual reference. It is a good idea to get them into the habit of looking to the board (or screen) for directions, as I believe you will find it to be a huge energy saver by not having to repeat directions.

- Meanwhile, as they are working quietly, you are clarifying the "Big Two": What is their lunch plan? How are they going home?

Meet the Teacher

- You have planned out an introduction for yourself, and when you are ready, you will begin with your very important first words. This sets the tone for whether or not they "get" to spend the year in your class or whether they are "stuck" with you. Talk about things that may interest them, but I recommend you do so with a tone of confident, pleasant command. Important: *You are not trying to be their friend here;* you are establishing yourself as their leader. Always stand before them with the presence of a leader.

- For me, in addition to sharing personal things with them so that they know who I am as a person, I always have my diplomas proudly hanging on the wall. I explain to them why I do that and that this year marks their progress toward that end. I explain to them that education is a free and beautiful gift for the mind that no one can take away. School is a huge privilege (explain why) and happens to be the law for good reason (invite conversation). Just like adults have jobs that they go to or businesses that they create and run, school is their job and their business, and today is day one. This is serious business, and I make it a priority to establish that tone. I promise them that I will not allow anyone to take away from their opportunity to learn (which plants the seeds for behavioral expectations). By the way, though I am serious in delivery, all of this is done with a friendly smile.

Side Note

- Elementary teachers should explain the procedure for using the restroom early in the day. Nerves do funny things to children. It only happened to me once, but I had a little boy wet his pants on the first day, and it ruined him for the rest of the year.

Establishing Community and Expectations

- Hold your first class meeting if this is part of what you want to establish, and I really hope it is. Class meetings are the heartbeat of my environment. (More on that in Truth #4 where we talk about the importance of establishing great relationships with your students.)

- Before anyone moves, don't forget to clearly explain and practice the procedures for transitioning to the meeting area, as you outlined in Step 2: Planning. Never assume that the students will politely and quietly do this without showing them how. All transitions will need to be modeled, practiced, and acknowledged.

- First group discussion question: *What kind of environment do you believe will help you learn best this year?* This accomplishes two things. It shows that you care about them, and it sets the stage for teamwork and collaboration. As a bonus, it gives them their first win (see below).

- After the discussion (record their suggestions on a poster if desired), explain that you hear them and that your classroom expectations (some say "rules") will be a direct result of that. Rejoice, because their idea of perfect is the same as yours! Now everyone is on the same page, and they feel like they were heard and understood (win). But be prepared for blurts. One time, I had a student at this point look disappointed at the proposed learning environment. He then blurted out, "But I'm the class clown!" I looked at him with a smile, and firmly stated, "We don't have class clowns." To which he exhaled, "Oh, good! That was a lot of work."

- Based on information gathered during the discussion of what they need in a great learning environment, inform them of your behavioral expectations (which, as mentioned, will magically line up). Now, this is a tricky subject, but I am going to share with you what has been my truth. I do not have a popular behavior plan or system in place that moves clips or gives check marks, punishes, or uses "money," or other rewards and prizes.

I do none of that. I have stayed far away from popular online applications, as well.

What would it mean to you to not have to deal with managing a complex, distracting, confusing, and interruptive behavior system? How much free time would that give you? If we are being honest, have those systems truly helped the children? Or does it consistently just point out the norm? (Surprise! Johnny's on red again and it's only 9 a.m.)

- Ideally, we want them to own their behavior and maintain self-control, which is a lifelong skill. We want to encourage them to do the right thing because it's the right choice, not because they will get a prize. I promise this is possible for you. I have freed myself of any time spent managing a behavior plan. It is a nonissue and nontopic in my classroom. Instead, I am clear about the expectations and tell them that their reward for expected behavior in my classroom is that they avoid consequences and gain self-respect.

- From day one, I am very clear with them that this is not a candy-and-stickers place. Instead, I tell them things like, "It is a grow-your-brain-and-love-each-other place. It is a community. It is your school family. We support each other, and we grow together. We are a team. You are a valuable part of that team. You will contribute to this community in a positive way. You will help others, and you will accept help. We will move together on everything."

You will come up with your own ideas and categories, but here is an example of what I explain to them:

Our Five Classroom Expectations

Every Day I Am:
1. Respectful
2. Responsible
3. Prepared
4. Proud
5. Kind

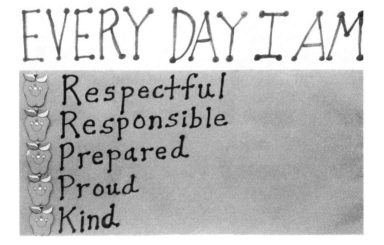

We clarify, together, the meaning of each of those words and give examples of what it might look like when it is working well, and what it looks like when it is off track.

Off-track examples might be:

Respectful: We discuss that any unwanted behavior or interruption to teaching and learning that comes up is not consistent with our expectation of respect.

Responsible: I might say something like, "Expecting parents or teachers to do things for you that you can do for yourself is not being responsible because you are a capable human being."

Prepared: We discuss that any missing assignment or material is not following our expectation of being prepared. We also talk about mental preparedness and the importance of having a healthy sleep schedule.

I then say, "It's really just those three things. If you are successful with those things, then you will..."

Proud: "...feel *proud* of yourself," which we define as having proper (not boastful) self-respect. "When you feel proud of yourself, you have an abundance of positive energy inside ready to burst out, and you are able to be..."

Kind: "...*kind* to others because you have enough to give. This will make you have a lot of friends and people will want to be around you because people appreciate those who are kind."

Summary: My overall message to the students is: "If you *are* respectful, responsible, and prepared, you will *feel* proud, and you will *be* kind. That is how you become successful in life. We are here to use our gifts and talents to give and serve, and these are your first steps toward that path. I will not allow anyone to take this away from you."

After our discussion, I eventually have my students create posters for each word to make sure everyone understands. These posters remain on the wall for the entire year. My older students are asked to write an essay based on their understanding of these expectations. Those are always fun to read!

Continue with Routines and Expectations

- I run the rest of the day like a regular workday, as previously mentioned, but with several stops for procedural explanations. For example, I had my third graders do multiplication and cursive their first day. They come in rested and hungry for work, so I take advantage of that. I don't think they waited all summer to do a maze, play bingo, or color a sheet. But that's just me; I'm not judging! In fact, I suggest, even on the first day, that you consider assigning homework. Again, they are ready and hungry to learn. Be sure that it is a task that they can do on their own without assistance and that it doesn't take too long. You want them to feel successful.

- Every single thing is done with a plan, so the day becomes an easy flow of what you have already rehearsed in your mind. The response to anything that comes up that wasn't planned for is, "I'm so glad that happened! Now we can talk about how we handle this…"

  That goes for behavior corrections as well. Don't be disrespectful about it, but don't tolerate anything outside of the boundaries. It is extremely important that any behavior that is not what you want to see all year gets corrected *immediately*. Let me repeat: Unless you want it, don't accept it. Redirect it. Correct it. Notice I am saying "redirect," "correct," but not "punish." Just politely smile and calmly, yet firmly, state: "I'm sorry, I must not have been clear. That behavior is not going to be acceptable in here." To which they usually say, "Okay," or if you're lucky, "Yes, ma'am." And for the vast majority, that is it! Many students will test you, but if you are confident, clear, and consistent, they will eventually get it, I promise.

- In all things, think: calm, clear, firm, and gentle. *Structure* is the name of the game, mixed with love and praise for their excellent ability to correctly perform the procedures. They should feel like they are impressing you. Tell them that they are! They should go home knowing they were the perfect student on their first day. In fact, when I taught younger students, I always sent a note (that I prewrote) to the parents bragging on their child. It said something simple like "____ had a great first day of school! ☺" Simple! Takes two seconds, and it means a lot to them.

Ending the Day

- Before dismissal, *rehearse the process for the next morning* (how they will enter, where they go, and what they do). The goal here is that you establish that they will enter the room and immediately get to work—not just tomorrow, but every single day. You will find that as they gently trickle in and seamlessly get settled, you are freed up to manage other things. This ends up becoming my favorite time of day. Those first 30 minutes end up feeling like I get extra planning time.

- Really think about what kind of routine you would like for the last few minutes of the day. Ending the day in a nurturing way works well for me. For my gifted students, I like to end the day on the carpet with brainteasers that they bring to class to share. This way I can relax and enjoy watching them think. For my elementary students, I sit in the rocking chair and read them a chapter in a book they love. This becomes my second favorite part of the day. Everything is calm and organized. They are packed up, the classroom is spotless (See

Truth #3, Brick #7 on the last 10 minutes), and everyone has had a great day.

Other Tips and Reminders:

- Procedures and routines must be easy to understand, and they must be given practice time to learn them.
- This means you have taken the time to clearly define for yourself exactly how your classroom will be run. If you haven't done this, you are setting the stage for undesired results, big time.
- Say, "*We* do it like this…"
- Say, "*It* works like this…"
- Rehearse, and correct with dignity.
- If something comes up prior to you stating the procedure, simply say, "I'm so glad this came up! Let's talk about how this works…"
- It's all about *training* and *consistency*. That's it.
- I strongly recommend no candy or other rewards. We are not rewarded in life for doing what is expected of us. That is not real life. Does the security guard at the airport give you a lollipop for standing in line and removing your shoes? Do you get a sticker for going the speed limit? Introduce them to reality.
- Expectations from a great leader are safer than rules from a dictator.

Important: All of the guidelines must be executed under the grand umbrella of LOVE. We are doing all of this because we care about them. We respect them as human beings. We want the best for them.

For those who may desire a visual of this to better understand, here you go:

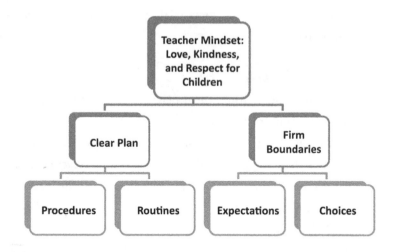

The results of this plan are that

- Students are safe, happy, and engaged.
- Students perform well on tests (because so much learning is able to take place).
- Students know they are respected and loved, even if they don't perform well.
- Students *want* to learn, and *want* to excel.
- Students become empowered as human beings.

Q: *That's great, Kerry, but what do I do when the kids are out of control? Let's be real, our students can't be perfect all of the time!*

My answer: You're right. They won't be. But everything is handled *right away*, which prevents it from escalating. If you stay consistent with your expectations (yes, they will test the boundaries) and remain firm in what you will and will not allow for the learning environment, they will get it. This is hard work, it doesn't just happen easily, but it is worth it.

Lead, Love, Learn

If you follow the guidelines laid out in this chapter, you and your students will thrive. You are setting up an environment of safety where love and firmness are established, and where students love to learn. Additionally, you are creating a space where actual personalized learning can take place. Instead of it being some fantasy, it can actually happen because once you have established order and routines, it just becomes a matter of strategic lesson planning and teaching.

Remember: environment first, lessons second.

Facilitating a businesslike learning environment frees you up to do the job you were hired for: teaching! What a concept. Stick to your vision, your routines, and your procedures, and you will *love teaching* because your students will *love learning*.

workload management

Truth #3: You Can Trade Your Bag of Bricks for a Bag of Tips

The key is not to prioritize what's on your schedule,
but to schedule your priorities.
—Stephen Covey

We have all heard the phrase, "Work smarter, not harder." Well, when it comes to teaching, sometimes you have to focus on doing both. It takes hard work, but it also calls for much harder work if you aren't working in a focused and streamlined manner. The truth is that lightening your workload will increase your sustainability, sanity, and overall happiness.

New teachers: Have any veteran teachers warned you that you'll sacrifice your personal life by entering into this profession? Experienced teachers: Do all of your friends know that you are beyond exhausted on Friday nights, to the point where they don't even call you to make plans? Does your family see you as two versions: school year version and summer version? Do you feel like you can never catch up with all of the things on your to-do list?

You are not alone if you answered "yes" to any of these questions.

Our local news recently did a segment on the results of a teacher survey sent out by the state superintendent of schools. Brenda Wood of *11 Alive* out of Atlanta, Georgia, reported, "Teachers feel like they are trying to take a drink out of a fire hose with the amount of demands that come at them." It's true. Teachers are asked to do so many things at once that it almost seems impossible to get anything done and still have a personal life.

Hang in There

After 20 years of teaching, I can tell you that it still feels like a lot on many days. From the first day of school to the last, with all of the constant activity, it sometimes feels like a nonstop circus. Only fellow colleagues understand what it is like to interact with hundreds of human beings starting very early in the morning, wear multiple hats, and feel like you are constantly being watched (you are) and listened to (you are) during the day. Once the students go home, your job is far from done. You likely have countless and endless email messages that are asking something of you; most likely you have to complete very strict paperwork trails on narrow time schedules and create organized lesson plans so that you can teach specified content to your students. Not to mention you have to finish what may feel like endless grading.

If it feels like a lot, it is! And it is normal and okay to feel overwhelmed. I have been there. To say that there were times that I was overwhelmed would be an understatement. Some years, I actually thought snow days saved me! But hoping for snow days is a ridiculous way to cope, especially if you live in Atlanta, Georgia. And looking forward to summers is even worse. Let's agree on one thing: Counting down the number of days to the next break is not a strategy that will offer you a life you love. But trading in your bricks for tips actually is. That is the focus of the rest of this chapter.

Now, the Good News: There Is a Better Way

The good news is that there is another way to operate, and there is a way to love teaching and still have a life. My hope for you is that you first embrace your life as a teacher, and then tweak things that are troubling you so that the load can become more manageable, and you can enjoy a balanced life.

It is possible. I promise.

How is this done?

I think everyone will find their own path for this process, but for me, I had to first get real about identifying the points of stress, and then figure out if I could control them. I had to ask myself: Is it even possible to change this? Is it actually possible to save time and energy so I can have a life outside of school, or am I a slave to the school year and can only be my energized self in the summer? And then finally, I had to make a change.

When I tried this technique, I learned something wonderful: It *is* possible to lighten things up, and if you do this, you will not be a slave to the school year or only have energy in the summer. There *are* ways to make teaching lighter and less demanding of our energy.

How to Start

Begin by identifying the point of stress, and then place your problem into the appropriate category.

You will find that most issues fall into one of three categories, each posing an important question to ask yourself.

1. **Avoidance Check:** Am I procrastinating?
2. **Lighten Up:** Am I taking things too seriously?
3. **Practical Thinking:** Is there a better way to do this?

Let's discuss each of these in detail:

Avoidance Check: *Am I procrastinating?*

Solution: If the thing that is driving you crazy is something that you must do, I lovingly advise you to stop the whining and complaining and just do it. We all are asked to do things that we don't want to do. Like I was told by my mentor and now tell my students, *do what you're supposed to do, when you're supposed to do it, whether or not you want to.* We all have to do things we don't want to do. It is part of life.

For example, recently there was mandatory online training for my district. It required that we watch several videos and submit written answers to questions to prove that we watched the videos. We all knew about it, and we all thought the same thing: "When do we have time for that?"

When I caught myself continuing to put it off, I realized I was wasting time thinking about it. It wasn't going away. The longer I waited didn't change it or make it magically disappear. It was still there.

I finally had to snap myself out of it and just do it. I think I dreaded and procrastinated about the task for a longer period of time than it took to actually complete it. When I finished, I wondered why I had waited so long. I had survived, it didn't kill me, and now I had one less thing to worry about.

Stop thinking about it so much! Like our friends at Nike say, "*Just do it.*" And then you can go home and put your slippers on.

Lighten Up: *Am I taking things too seriously?*

Solution: Ask yourself, in the big picture of life, is it really that big of a deal? Will this matter in a month? In a year? If not, lighten up and let it go. Let's not make too much of the little things in life.

Another thing to ask is: *Can you find any humor in it at all?* Try not to take things so seriously. It can be quite liberating! When I was in undergraduate school, one of my professors had us keep a humor journal. This professor was fighting cancer and had nutritionally beaten it. He was an absolute role model for us on how to live each and every day as if it were important, and as if it were our last. He encouraged us to write down things that we found funny or things we read that made us laugh.

I'd like to encourage you to start your own humor journal dedicated to the funny things that happen during the school day. If you can't find humor in the task itself, look to the students to release some laughter. You know what I'm talking about. Kids are hilarious!

Here are a few to get you started:

- Last year, a fellow teacher wrote, "Do #1-10" on the board. A student asked, "What does hashtag 1-10 mean?"
- It had been a while since my teacher friend had colored her hair and a student asked, "Mrs. M., do you know that your hair is two different colors? It's turning brown!"

- During some history research, I was watching a student of mine look at some old black-and-white video clips. She was in awe. She looked at me and said, "It must have been so boring to only wear black or white. When did color get invented?"
- From a second grader: "I have to keep my hair cut short because if it gets long, it gives me bad dreams."
- From a kindergartener: "I feel sad today because my dog is having surgery." I told him that I understood. He continued, "Yeah, my mom wants to make sure that he doesn't get married."

Enjoy your time with these precious sweethearts, and always maintain a sense of humor. It is good to keep your energy playful and light as much as possible. Go ahead and let yourself enjoy them!

If your problem does not fall into one of the above-mentioned categories, then it might be a practical issue that may benefit from some creative problem solving.

Practical Thinking: *Is there a better way to do this?*

Solution: You are going to have to experiment here to find things that work for you, because everybody is different and all teaching assignments are not the same. I will give you some of my personal examples here to get you going, but what I'd really like for you to do is make a list of all of the things that drive you crazy. Then, pick one to make into a balloon. Think to yourself: How can I make this lighter? Sometimes we just need to take the time to think it through.

The problem with teaching is that our days are so intense and so busy that it is challenging to accomplish this. Only fellow teachers understand what it's like to be "on" all day, and go from one thing to the next without stopping. There is so much stimulation that things will never change unless we take time outside of school to think things through. Trust me, it will be worth it. Be disciplined about carving out time for this. You could do this exercise on a Saturday morning with a cup of coffee, tea, or hot chocolate.

Ask: Is there one thing I can do differently? What change can I make?

I'm not talking about spending hours and hours looking for an answer to your problems on the Internet. The answers to your problems are likely not found in another workbook or website or worksheet. The answers that work best are within you.

Tip: Don't be afraid to admit what is not working. It is the first step to improving it.

So with that said, let's take the time to practically discuss how to shift the heavy weight created by the bricks in your life to something more airy (lighter) and much more manageable. To that end, it is time to shift some bricks into balloons.

From Bricks to Balloons

Whether I was new to teaching or new to a position, there always seemed to come a point where it felt like the load was too much. When I realized that I was losing my personal life and couldn't continue with the pace, I decided that if this was a practical problem, I was going to do something about it.

I tried some things, and they didn't work. I tried others, and they did work. Eventually, with each new year of experience and each new trial and error, I watched each heavy brick in my bag get transformed into a balloon. I addressed each heavy burden that I carried with a strategy and made it lighter and easier. You will come up with your own, but here are some that worked for me:

From Brick to Balloon #1: Grading

Brick: Too much grading! I was spending nights and weekends grading papers. I started to dread Sundays worst of all, because that day was spent trying to catch up before another week of more papers started.

Balloon: I began prioritizing what needed to be "graded" and what could be "checked." I realized that not everything needs a grade.

The big idea for me changed when I switched my thinking from *what is their score,* to *who needs help?* Then, I started making two piles: those who understand, and those who need assistance. That cut my grading down significantly. But then I thought: Why am I spending so much time doing this? Isn't there some other way to sort through papers?

Then it dawned on me: *Why can't we go over these papers as a group?* Why can't I call out the correct answers while the students check their work? I was hesitant to start this because I wasn't sure if it was technically allowed, but what I discovered is that it became so instructionally valuable that I would never teach another day without using this strategy.

Sometimes they would correct their own papers, and sometimes they would switch papers with a partner. I found that it was best if they were looking at their own paper because then they could ask questions on the spot about misunderstandings. Or, I could glance around quickly and see where the problems were and give a quick personalized tutorial.

From Brick to Balloon #2: Extra Talk

Brick: They won't stop talking! Why is there constant chatter?

Balloon: The best thing I ever did was to require whisper voices if we were working independently. But this was impossible when they were doing group work. I realized that if I let it go just a little bit, it would snowball. What would start as nice student collaboration would sometimes pile into a whole lot of noise, making it hard for anyone to think.

So, I learned the simple skill of politely nipping it in the bud, starting with the first day of school, as mentioned in Truth #2. As soon as the noise level crept toward unacceptable, I would address it. Right away! No exceptions. It took practice, but every year my students learned where the line was, and they would tone it down even without me saying anything. Be consistent, and they will surprise you.

From Brick to Balloon #3: Classroom Interruptions

Brick: I was feeling frustrated that so many students would interrupt the room by asking to get a drink, use the restroom, etc. I first tried to let them excuse themselves by putting a pass on their desk. This worked well when my classroom was self-contained, but it got tricky when I changed positions and instead had classes come and go all day.

Balloon: To eliminate this problem, I taught my students to communicate using a secret sign language. For example, one raised finger meant, "May I please use the restroom?" to which I would nod yes if it was an appropriate time. This allowed for movement around the room in a way that did not interrupt or disturb anyone. Plus, it helped me keep track of who was in the room and who wasn't in the event of a fire drill or other emergency.

From Brick to Balloon #4: "I'm Done. Now What?"

Brick: It's every teacher's nightmare when students ask, "What do we do when we're done?" or "I'm done. Now what should I do?"

Balloon: I required students to have three books on their desks in the corner at all times: one nonfiction, one fiction, and one free choice. This way, if an emergency came up, if they finished something early, or if they didn't know what to do, they would "pull their book."

Each book had a purpose, and once a month they would do thematic book reports on one of them. This approach resulted in zero down time, an enhanced love of reading, and accelerated reading scores for all of the years that I taught general education. My class won reading awards seven years in a row utilizing this technique!

It naturally became the go-to activity whenever they sat down in their seat. After entering class in the morning, after returning to class from specials or lunch, etc., they knew to "pull their book." This gave me a couple of minutes to regroup myself, and it eliminated the need to rush right into a lesson worried they would start acting up if I didn't. It also served as the best task for the students to engage in if I was called away to handle an unexpected situation.

From Brick to Balloon #5: Organization

Brick: My students were only keeping their desks clean when they suspected that the Desk Fairy might be coming (elementary teachers know what I'm talking about).

Balloon: I decided to change things and make it become an expectation that their desks remain organized. And things that are expected are not rewarded.

Warning: This needs to be taught! They do not automatically know the skill of how to organize.

We started with a discussion to make a plan for all items in the desk. We decided to put hardcover books on one side, softcover books on the other, create a tunnel in the middle for crayons and a pencil pouch, and put two pencils in front with a red pen and a highlighter.

Then, we learned how to stop and organize every day. We would acknowledge that it is okay that it gets messy while we work, but at the end of the day, we know we have to regroup and clean.

It literally took them less than two minutes every day to check their desk. For some, it never got messy because they had a place for everything.

Even though all of their desks end up looking the same, I found that providing structure in this area lightened the load on the students because they no longer had to stress out about where things were. They could quickly and easily transition from one subject to the next without skipping a beat. This strategy works well for organizing binders, and upper grade students could benefit from these "stop and organize" checkpoints. It's amazing how much time is saved by knowing where everything goes and where everything can be found quickly. (Hint, hint: This tip isn't just for students!)

From Brick to Balloon #6: Wasted Time

Brick: I was cramming everything I had to do into after-school time, and I was feeling like I was wasting moments during the day.

Balloon: I was right. I was wasting precious moments. I learned that I could multitask some things throughout the day. If I carefully structured the day, I could get a lot done in between things.

For example, if I planned an independent assignment directly following a spelling test, I could quickly grade the spelling test immediately after.

If I had a spot near the door where I put things that needed to be copied, I could grab the pile as we walked to specials, and I could go directly to the copier instead of coming back to the room first.

As they were cleaning up their desks during the last 10 minutes of the day (more on this below), I could be cleaning up mine at the same time. By making a plan and using my time wisely at key moments throughout the day, I left only tasks that required great concentration for the end of the day, best done in an empty classroom.

From Brick to Balloon #7: Chaotic Beginnings

Brick: The first 10 minutes of my day were making me crazy. I felt like I was walking into chaos and confusion every morning.

Balloon: I decided to declare that the first 10 minutes of the day were going to be the last 10 minutes of the day before.

I decided that every day before I left school, I would spend 10 focused minutes getting everything set for the next day. Desk clean, lesson plans organized and out, sticky note with to-do list next to the computer, etc.

This way, when I walked in, it would feel peaceful and calm. I didn't have to remember where I was or what to do because it was already done and organized.

I learned to do this with my students as well. The last 10 minutes of *their* day were the first 10 minutes of the next. They spent the last 10 minutes of class cleaning and organizing for the next day, including pencil sharpening. It is an "all skate," and everyone contributes to making the classroom look as nice as it did in the morning. I once had a parent stand outside of my classroom in awe watching this happen. She later told me that she had no idea her child knew how to clean like that!

From Brick to Balloon #8: Hunger Games

Brick: I realized I was either starving or stuffed throughout the school day. I would feel starving when my lunch period was late in the day, and then when it did come, I would stuff myself sick in those 20 minutes!

Balloon: I decided to invest in a mini-fridge for my classroom. It was the best thing I ever did. I stocked it with easy to eat things like carrots, apple slices, turkey, string cheese, protein shakes, and water. This way I could snack throughout the entire day, or eat in more reasonable intervals and amounts so that chemically I wasn't uncomfortable.

I found out that I am in a much better mood when I am well fed. Go figure! Because I paid attention to my natural hunger patterns, many times my lunch period would become an extra mini planning period to get things done. (Or a time to take a nap on my desk. Just kidding!)

From Brick to Balloon #9: Managing My Feelings

Brick: When I was having a bad day, I would blame myself and beat myself up when I got home. It would ruin the evening.

Balloon: Instead of bottling up my frustrations, I decided to create a mini private vent. I decided to acknowledge my frustrations in the moment, and give them permission to be expressed.

This solution might seem silly, and I am a little embarrassed to share it, but sometimes our solutions only make sense to us, and that is all that matters. No judging!

Here is what I did. I hung a blank piece of chart paper on the back of my closet door and wrote in a secret language that only I understood. For example, if I was feeling it bubble inside and there were several more hours left in the day with a roomful of students and

I knew I was getting close to losing it, I would quickly open my closet door, write TDISA! and then get back to the kids with a smile. (That stood for THIS DAY IS SO ANNOYING!) See—better already, right? Worked for me.

From Brick to Balloon #10: "Save the World" Mentality

Brick: I felt weighed down with the burden of wishing I could help each and every student and was stressed out about the low babies that didn't seem to budge in progress.

Balloon: I had to realize that I am human and cannot save everyone. However, I can encourage everyone to live up to their full potential in life.

In that spirit, I began encouraging and complimenting *efforts* more than outcomes. It became my personal goal to inspire each student to do their personal best, whatever that was, and to love and accept them for whatever that was.

Recognizing Your Own Bricks

What about you? Consider the bricks that you are carrying around. Did any of the aforementioned bricks remind you of some things that burden you? It doesn't have to be just for school-related things. Maybe you are feeling burdened by something going on in your personal life. That's okay! You are a real person with a real life. What's important is that you have the courage to admit the challenge, and then practice your problem-solving skills.

Why not start now? Use the following template to begin your own personal quest to trade bricks for balloons. There is no wrong answer, and no one is judging you. Try something, if it doesn't work, try something else. You'll get there! You'll find what works. Give it a try!

_____

Why It Matters

The goal of this Truth is to reduce your load so that you can enjoy a more balanced life. This matters because *you* matter and you deserve to be happy, no matter what you do. Putting things in the proper perspective will help you organize your burdens, and by applying time and energy-saving strategies, you can lighten the load and love teaching.

Remember, first decide which category your problem falls into. Then, see if there is a way to solve it that makes sense for you. Try something. If it works, great. If not, try something else.

Not everything can be made perfect, but I believe that if you regularly trade your bricks for balloons, you will be well on your way to freeing up time and energy. This will allow you to have a life you love that includes some time for hobbies after school. You need it, you deserve it, and it *is* possible. Tennis, anyone?

people management

Truth #4: All Relationships Matter

*The most important single ingredient in the formula
of success is knowing how to get along with people.*
—**Theodore Roosevelt**

Joy, Support, and Impact—It's All about Relating

did you know that as teachers, people management is just as important as classroom management? When I first became a teacher, everyone told me about the importance of classroom management, which I quickly learned was true. Without classroom management, your classroom is a world of chaos. However, they didn't warn me about the importance of *people* management: the ability to get along with lots of different types and groups of people, and how to create relationships with them. After years of teaching experience, I can say that it is a fact that your ability to get along with others matters a lot! You will encounter and be expected to manage people of all types and ages. And at the end of the day, if you do not learn these skills, you will not enjoy teaching.

The Art of People Management

I learned very quickly that I had to deal with lots and lots of people throughout the day—all ages, all backgrounds, all family dynamics, and all roles. From those looking up to me for guidance (students), to those who look after those looking up to me for guidance (parents), to those who are in a supervisory role (administrators), and to those who are doing the same thing that I am but with a different audience (colleagues). How does one manage it all?

The current hurdle is that as educators, we are not taught how to be in the business of people management, yet that is what we will spend most of our time doing. It is also the most important part of your role as a teacher. Relationships are the fabric of our life, as they represent a basic and fundamental human connection. Your ability to get along with people will directly impact the level of success you have in this profession, as well as your level of joy, support, and overall impact as a teacher.

Joy: the extent to which we find pleasant satisfaction in what we are doing.

Support: the extent to which we help others, and others have a willingness to help us.

Impact: the extent to which we leave a lasting impression.

Isn't that what we all want as teachers? Don't we want to make a difference, be supported, and enjoy our life in this profession? Of course we do, and making that happen is all about relating. If we are unable to relate well to other human beings, all of those areas will suffer. However, if we are able to relate well to other human beings, all of those areas will flourish. I am committed to giving you the information you need to be successful in this area of relating, so please read on!

Relating 101

When examining relationships, we usually don't think about them until something goes wrong. For example, if we are getting along well with people we care about, it doesn't seem to register as being all that important. However, if something goes wrong in a relationship with someone else, it bothers us. It makes us feel "off" and uncertain. This is true for our family relationships, our personal relationships, and it's true for those relationships we have at school.

Have you ever had a day that was going really well, only to have it be ruined by a school relationship problem? Perhaps a student suddenly challenged you, or an administrator questioned you on something and you felt misunderstood. Or maybe you checked your email during your lunch break and opened it up to find an angry email from a parent. All of these examples are enough to throw anyone's day off.

While we can't always avoid altercations, we can learn to be better equipped to deal with them by learning to better relate. Doing so will lower the amount of relationship problems we experience, and allow us to effectively and quickly deal with them when they do arise. By the end of this section, you will have everything you need to create successful relationships in your school world. Let's start by looking at the relationships you will encounter.

As a teacher, you will be managing four main relationship groups:

1. Students
2. Parents
3. Administrators
4. Colleagues

You might have questions such as:

- How do I connect with my students when I have so many?
- How do I handle an irate parent?
- How do I keep my administrators pleased with me?
- How do I get along with my colleagues, even if we don't see eye to eye?

All of these questions will be answered in this section, but more importantly, you are going to find the tips and tools you need to establish *positive relationships* with all four groups of people. We will explore each type of relationship in detail: The first two relationships, students and parents, are the most important, and we will spend the majority of our time together on those. Then we will look at top tips for creating great relationships with administrators and colleagues.

Students

Our relationship with our students sets the tone for their entire learning experience. It is the backdrop of the classroom and the culture in which everyone must exist. For that reason, it is the most important relationship you will have.

Our ability to connect with our students will coincide with our potential to have an impact and make a lasting impression. If our students know that we care about them and respect them as human beings, they will be inspired from within to engage and learn.

Our relationship with our students begins the moment we meet them. We should never underestimate the power of a first impression. It's fairly well known that people form almost instant opinions about each other within seconds of engagement. This does not just apply to adults—it is person to person, which means it applies to you and your students. So, how do we ensure that we make the best first impression possible? It starts with becoming aware of our body language and tone. We always want to be sure that we are looking students in the eye, have a calm and pleasant tone of voice, and treat them in a respectful and humane way at all times. Then, we begin cultivating two layers of relationship with them: leader of the class and personal.

In many ways these two roles are one in the same. As a student observes us leading the whole class in a respectful way, he or she will feel respected on a personal level. Similarly, when a student sees us giving personal attention to a classmate and really caring for their needs, he or she feels safe and happy about having us as his or her classroom leader. As you can see, classroom leadership and personal relationships go hand in hand.

The opposite is also true. If our students observe us losing it, or going off on another student, they will not feel safe as an individual. They will worry and think that they are next. Or, if they are an older student, they may get excited at the opportunity to challenge us. Either way, watching any teacher lose control makes students feel unstable, and as a result, they will internally start to harbor disrespect for that teacher. And it only takes one slip up for the relationship to change. They will not forget. So we must do everything we can to ensure this never happens. The good news is we know the importance of maintaining kindness, consistency, and composure in our relationships with students. As long as we keep that in mind at all times, we are building successful student-teacher relationships.

In addition to remaining kind, consistent, and composed, there are four other main ways that I establish relationships with students both as the leader of the class and on a personal level: class meetings, student letters, three-second comments, and ten-second conferences. Let's look over each one in detail.

1. Class Meetings

If you teach elementary school, I strongly recommend connecting with your students through class meetings. I have been utilizing this technique to create community for over 18 years, and I would never do it any other way. We begin in a circle, either on the carpet or in chairs, and we allow each person the opportunity to speak. We might share something that has been going on in our personal lives, or something about ourselves that helps the other classmates get to know us better. It is our time together to make connections and support each other. It is through these meetings that we create a family-like atmosphere.

When the students feel safe and comfortable, they are not afraid to mention that their parents are divorcing and they feel sad or that they recently learned their uncle has cancer. They also share positive life experiences such as winning a sports event or taking music lessons. It is our way of remembering that there is a whole life that exists outside of school, and we cannot entirely separate the two. I always encourage students to be vulnerable with what is going on, so that we can practice problem-solving skills, exercise compassion, and experience empathy. It helps them feel understood and cared for.

We also discover in our meetings points of conversation to develop friendships with one another. For example, if Joey told us about his new puppy during the class meeting and a student is curious about it, I would encourage that student to ask him more about it at lunch or recess. This gives students a reason to engage one on one and form their own relationships with each other. Class meetings are definitely the heartbeat of my classroom environment, and I have had many students come back to me years later saying that it was the part of my class that they loved the most.

If you teach upper grades, this concept could still be practiced in a modified way. Once a month on a Friday, for example, you could take a portion of class for this very impactful practice. I have found that most meetings take just 10 minutes, after which it would be up to you to lead a discussion or life lesson about anything that arose. You could even begin by posing a question, and creating a Socratic seminar-type atmosphere.

If the class size is too large to realistically entertain this concept, try thinking outside of the box. Could the class be split in half? Could there be four group rotations, and one of them is in a circle with you? One thing I'd like to challenge you to do as you journey through teaching is to stay open to possibilities. When other teachers around you are saying, "Oh, I could never do that," or "That would never work for me," I want you to activate your creative brain and ask yourself, "*How* can it work for me?"

Students of all ages want to be accepted and acknowledged as human beings, not just as a person who sits behind a desk; these meetings allow you to create another layer of connection and compassion in the classroom. Give them a try, and I am sure you will see they go a long way in building successful relationships for all involved.

2. Student Letters

Written communication is a beautiful thing. Some students will communicate in writing feelings that they would never say out loud. In order to get to know my students and help them feel heard, I always begin each year by asking them to write me a letter. We take a portion of the first class (approximately 15 minutes), and students compose their messages. I ask them to help me get to know them. For example, what are their interests, hobbies, and concerns? How do they like to learn? What are their hopes for the year? Is there anything that they want me to know about them? I am always pleasantly surprised at the openness and courage that many students exhibit. Some stick to the basics, and some choose to go deep and get real. This year, I had a student say in her letter:

> sister. My parents are divorced. I see my dad every other weekend. My art is in a museum. My mom has crones disease. If you see me cry its because I either miss my mom or I am upset about my life. My life is hard. I sometimes have to be the mom. I

I'm sure you can imagine how that letter struck my heart. Always remember that your students are dealing with real life issues, and the best thing you can do is accept them as they are, and make them feel safe, supported, and loved for the time you are together. Give your students a chance to express themselves in writing, as it may provide unforeseen opportunities for connection.

This practice doesn't have to be just at the beginning of the year. I also have them write reflection letters at the end of units or grading periods. What went well? What have they been learning? What could have been better? What else would they like to tell me? I am always amazed at their transparency and trust.

Recently, a student told me in her letter that she did something bad, but she didn't want to tell her parents for fear of upsetting them. She said that she had ripped a gem (bead) off her shirt the previous day, and accidentally stuck it in her ear too far and couldn't get it out! When I spoke with her about it, she confessed to me, crying, that she was in a lot of pain and couldn't hear out of that ear. I told her that I was so proud of her for having the courage to tell me, and that we would make sure she was okay and that she would not be in trouble. In having the privilege of helping her through that situation, she got the care that she needed and deserved, and I felt like I made a difference that day. Win-win. All because of letters.

3. Three-Second Comments

Another way to connect with your students is by regularly giving them positive verbal comments. I have always found that writing comments on papers, though extremely valuable as it relates to their work, isn't always timely and doesn't always address those "in progress" moments that help us connect with them. But *speaking* the comments only takes seconds and creates more of an immediate interpersonal experience. Think of these as tiny acknowledgments that help create a *culture of care*.

Let's look at some examples. As you pass by a student, you could say things (with a smile) like:

- That's looking great!
- You are on the right track!
- How did your performance go last night? (This models following up on things mentioned in class meetings. It shows that you care about them as a human being, not just as a student.)
- I'm proud of all of the effort you are putting into this assignment.
- How did you come up with that idea? It's fascinating!
- I see that you have stopped your work. Do you need help?
- Is everything okay? (Always treat them with dignity, even if the problem seems silly.)

- I like the way you…
- Thank you for…
- I notice…
- I appreciate…

All of these are ways to let the students know that you notice them, you care about them, and you accept them. We want to be sure we are saying these positives over and over, so that they know we care, and when a negative issue requires attention, it will be better received.

4. Ten-Second Conferences

I started doing these around year three, and I've never stopped. This is a mini-conference you have with each individual student, and it literally only takes an average of 10 to 30 seconds. Here, you will be calling students over to you (away from the other students for privacy) and asking them how everything is going for them. I do this very early in the year (within the first two weeks), and then again later in the year, or as I sense the need. Look at this as a quick check-in. Most students will say that everything is fine, but once in a while I will find that a student, when provided that safe space and opportunity, will confess to something that is bothering him or her. For example, it might be that they are still struggling with a learning concept, or it might be that someone in another class is being really mean to them at recess. An upper grade student might admit that his or her homework has been problematic, that they don't know how to organize themselves, or that they are feeling a lot of pressure. It is our responsibility as leading adults in their lives to be aware of their well-being.

We spend more time with some of them than their parents do, and we need to become cognizant and informed of what may be stumbling blocks in their lives. Once we acquire this information, it is our duty to help them overcome the obstacles. While this may not be in the fine print of your teaching contract, these opportunities are where you can truly make a lasting impact in the lives of your students. Take the time to check-in and lend a helping hand.

I have found that through these four practices, we can create meaningful and memorable relationships with our students. It is through these bonds that the students feel safe, acknowledged, cared for, and valued. And the truth is, they do matter! They are the reason we show up to school every day, and they are the reason for our devotion. Always nurture and protect your relationships with your students as your most important connection.

Of course, there would be no students without parents, which is why the next most important relationship is with the parental figures.

Parents

This relationship is going to vary immensely depending on the type of school at which you teach. I have taught in schools where the parent component is nonexistent, where it is beyond important, and where it is someplace in between. Regardless, your efforts should remain the same. If you teach at a school where the parents are not involved, never come to conferences, and you never hear from them or see them, please continue to communicate with them, keep them informed, and invite them in. They might surprise you some day, and if not, at least you made an effort.

In those situations, I would also encourage you to remain compassionate about what your students' home life must be like, and focus extra attention on them. It has been my experience when I've taught at these types of schools that this extra focus made my relationships with my students even stronger. With every effort that might have been redirected toward a parent, I found that I was freed up to concentrate on the students and love them even more.

I had an entire classroom filled with this type of student during my first year teaching. Every day brought another story from another student about some outrageous thing going on at home. Whether it was Michael who constantly talked about the drugs his older brother was doing or Paula who would cry and beg me not to tell her parents that she didn't turn in a project on time. She was sent into a near panic attack at the thought of letting them down.

These were rough kids from rough homes. And while invitations were abundant, I never saw the parents. These poor 10- and 11-year-olds were put through more than any of us could imagine.

But you know what? For *our* time together, it was love. In *our* classroom, it was the opportunity to learn. For *our* space, they were accepted.

On the last day of school at dismissal, instead of racing down the hallway for summer freedom as we all would expect, my heart quickly sank. They wouldn't leave. Buses were being called, but they wouldn't go. They hugged their desks and said, "I don't want to go home."

I don't think I've ever cried so hard after having to insist they go. I sat in my empty classroom wondering what they were going home to and wishing I could take it all away for them. You may experience similar circumstances, so prepare your heart. Remember, if you don't have involved parents, love your students even harder. They need it more than anyone.

However, at most schools, you are going to need to learn to create positive relationships with the parents of your students. They will always want to know that you care about their child and that you are competent in your practice. They also want to know that you are there for them if they have a concern and that you will promptly address their concerns.

I learned a long time ago that a happy student equals happy parents. My goal is always to send home a happy, well-educated child. I do this by being hyperaware of my students and by creating authentic connections, as described previously. If I am in tune with the students, I can (hopefully) see when they are unhappy or not getting something, and through ongoing informal assessments (made easy; don't forget the bricks to balloons), I can quickly assess and address their learning needs.

As for the parents, strive to see things from their perspective. Fundamentally, parents want to know:

Is my child safe?
Is my child heard?
Is my child cared about?
Is my child learning?
Is my child challenged?
Is my child happy?
Does my child have friends?
Is my child performing at their potential?
Are there any problems with my child academically or socially?

This may seem like a lot of questions and a lot of responsibility, but don't worry. Generally, I have found that parents are easy to handle if you have a good relationship with your students, making that your priority. Additionally, I recommend these four tips for establishing great relationships with parents.

1. Parent Inventory

The first thing I do to establish a relationship with my parents is send home a questionnaire at the beginning of the year. I call it a "Parent Inventory," but I've heard it called other things. It is similar to the letter

I ask the students to write, except this version is more direct. It is a short paper that asks questions about their child, any hopes or concerns they have for the year, how I can best support their child, and anything else that would be helpful for me to know. It is an opportunity for parents to feel heard, and it gives an instant impression that you care about them, you care about their child, and you want the absolute best results for your time together. Who would object to that?

2. Communicate Caring

The next thing I would recommend is to communicate regularly and promptly. Keeping them informed of classroom happenings and curriculum matters is important. I found that a weekly newsletter or occasional email was the easiest for me, but you may have your own approach, such as posting things on a website or school purchased portal. You will find what works for you and your teaching style.

While simple newsworthy items are important, of even greater importance is to simply let them know you care. It is the number one thing you can do for parents. Let them know by the things you say and the things you do. For example, if a parent has sent you a flaming email and you do not respond to it for days, you are communicating that you do not care enough to take the time to send a one-minute email that says, "Thank you for your email. I will be back in touch soon with a response." Even if you can't address the concern right away, send a courtesy reply letting them know they've been heard and you will be in touch. If not, you can expect that they will go straight to the administration, and then it's all downhill from there.

Ideally, you want to resolve all student and parent issues without having to involve administration. This is to be expected, and your principal will most likely make it clear to all parents that their first step is to talk to you if there is an issue, not to them. I had an administrator tell me that 95 percent of his problems went away when he strictly gave up intervening on behalf of parents. We want that! We want for our principal to be freed up to do his or her job and not have to deal with parent complaints. It is not a wise use of their time.

Generally, it is expected (and strongly recommended) that you remain the direct communicator with the parents. Make it clear that you are open and that no problem should go to the administrators without you having knowledge of it or without you being given the chance for resolution. We will discuss this point further below in our section on administrators. Overall, in my experience, direct communication with parents is the quickest and most effective route to resolving any questions, issues, or concerns.

3. Remain Courteous and Professional, No Matter What

It is extremely important to always remain professional in your communications. You do not want to be that teacher who has a reputation of being short or cruel to parents. Be careful. Anything you say, write, or do, will be held against you in the administrator's office. I have seen this time and time again with my colleagues. A parent will come to school with printouts of emails and show them to the principal demanding a change in classroom placements, ruining that teacher's reputation.

I cannot stress enough that teachers must establish professional and courteous relationships with parents and maintain that standard at all times. Everyone is on the same team. Everyone wants what is best for the child. Always keep that in mind.

You may now be thinking, "Yes, Kerry, but what about the irate parent who is screaming in your face and accusing you of ruining their child?" Trust me, I've been there. You will not be able to join the official "Real Teacher Club" until you have had this experience (I'm kidding). But it is very likely to happen to you, no matter how great of a teacher you are. So, it is best to be prepared. I am going to first suggest how to handle it and then tell you about the time it happened to me.

If you ever find yourself in this uncomfortable situation, first and foremost, remain calm. Remain composed and professional, even if your instinct is to retaliate and defend yourself. Then, simply state something like, "I am happy to have a conversation about this if we are both able to communicate in a professional and respectful manner. Otherwise, we will need to reschedule." It is of utmost importance that you do not allow yourself to be treated inappropriately. Do not engage if you feel any aggression or overt rudeness. If they do not leave, buzz the office for help or go to the teacher next door for support. Stay calm and in control.

When it happened to me, my approach was slightly different than described above. You will find the approach that works for you; just make sure you have a plan!

One of the hardest students I ever taught had a grandmother who was part of our faculty, and she was a helicopter grandmother (always hovering). She was dissatisfied with absolutely everything I did and insisted that her grandson's problems were my fault. One day after school, she came into my room flaming mad and went off on a screaming tangent about all of the things I did wrong. I was caught off guard. About halfway through her rant, I realized what was happening and decided to stand strong. I kept a perfectly calm and attentive face during this episode and waited for the moment in which I would have a chance to respond.

When she finally finished, I simply and calmly said with a slight smile, "Is there anything else you would like to say that would be helpful?" She became tongue-tied and embarrassed at this unexpected response, apologized profusely, and left the room. Our boundaries were set, and I never heard from her again.

The mother of the above child confronted me once, as well. One day after school, she cornered me in my classroom and had a similar attack toward me (the apple doesn't fall far from the tree). For her, my approach was slightly different. When she finished, I explained to her that I was confused. I told her that in my long history of teaching, I have always had great relationships with parents. I couldn't understand where the divide was coming from with her, and I remained open to her suggestions on how to bridge the gap. I reminded her that we were on the same team, and that we both wanted the best for her child. I established that I was not the enemy and asked how I could help her feel comfortable. I was totally calm and respectful.

She then started crying and explained that they had just received really hard news from the doctor, who had diagnosed her son with an unexpected disorder. She was scared, and it was coming through as blame. I gave her a hug, and our relationship was immediately repaired.

Always be aware that there could be more going on than you realize. Keep your composure, remain calm, and react with kindness. If you do fall short on your side, have the courage to admit it, apologize, and recover. We are all human, and we are all doing the best that we can.

And finally…

4. Re-Think Conferences

Although every school has set conference times, I approach this slightly differently. In addition to making a set conference time available to parents if they so desire, I inform them that my doors are open year-round, at any time, for any reason. Although I invite, I do not require a conference. (Warning: Your school may be different. Follow the expectations of your principal.)

Parents are busy! And honestly, so am I. If they are coming in to have a conference, I am going to make sure it is worthy of their time and mine. Has anyone else had seven back-to-back conferences during conference days? It becomes a blur after a while. Instead, I strive for authentic connections with each parent, where we talk about their child all around. If there is a concern, they know that I will be prompt in my communication. As a result, the parents learn to trust me. In the meantime, I tell them no news equals good news, and I assure them that they will never be surprised by anything. If their child is getting anything other than an A, we will talk. I tell them to keep up the good work! Managing my conferences with an open-door policy allows for more authentic communication and connection with parents, and it benefits the students as well. I highly recommend you adopt this win-win strategy.

All of these approaches have worked well for me over the years, so I encourage you to try them out and experiment with others, ultimately finding a system that works for you. I can say with confidence that by inviting feedback early on, communicating regularly and professionally, and by making the most of conferences, you will have great relationships with parents. Establishing positive relationships with the parents of your students creates the best chance of getting that child over the net, together. Remember, everyone is on the same team.

Now that we have discussed students and parents, let's turn our focus to administrators.

Administrators

Having a positive relationship with your administrators is of utmost importance for an enjoyable teaching experience. If you get along well with your administrators, your life will be a lot easier. If you cause problems for them or otherwise challenge their decisions, be ready for a miserable existence. This section will outline my top tips for nurturing this important relationship.

The first thing to remember about your administrators is that they care about you and want you to be successful and happy. But don't forget that you are not their only concern. They have the weight of the entire school upon them. For all of the pressure that you feel in your classroom, multiply that many times over to get an idea of what they might feel.

For example, in addition to overseeing the school's staffing, instructional plan, and day-to-day operations, the principal also plays a key role in setting and realizing a strategic vision and improvement plan for the school. They are the ones that the district looks to for enrollment, student performance, and community reputation. They have pressure from superintendents, parents, school boards, and the community at large. They also spend an enormous amount of time managing the budget. Do you better understand why handling your own problems might be of benefit for this relationship?

I have always made it my practice to leave the principal alone unless it was something that required their awareness, input, or permission. If you are new to a school, or even if you are not, don't bother the admin office with things you can handle without them. Ask your mentor or ask a colleague before you go marching into their office about something. Just as you do not prefer an unannounced parent showing up in your room, respect their office space with the same regard.

Aside from having to manage incompetent or irresponsible staff (don't let that be you), an administrator's biggest time waster is dealing with student discipline or parent complaints. They should not have to deal with things that you could and should be managing. To avoid problems, be sure to establish a firm but loving classroom management plan as described in Truth #2, and establish relationships with students and parents as described in this section. This will ensure that there are procedures in place and that students are too busy and engaged to misbehave. Should there be an issue, you can communicate directly with the parents and resolve the problem quickly and effectively.

If you handle your parents with the care previously described, your parents should not be going to administrators with concerns, and you should avoid difficult relationships with either parents or principals. Just to be sure, I would encourage you to communicate this information to your administrators early on. You can even put it in an email at the start of the year. Something like:

Dear Administrators,

I just wanted to let you know that I will be communicating to my parents that if they have any concerns or issues throughout this school year, their first line of communication should be with me. In the unlikely event that a parent from my classroom approaches you with a concern this year, please kindly ask them, "Have you spoken to the classroom teacher yet?" and if they haven't, please redirect them, and I will gladly handle it.

Sincerely,

Teacher

Imagine the smile of relief that you just gave your administrators! That is what we want to achieve. Don't burden them with problems that you can easily solve.

Here are some other tips to having a great relationship with your administrators:

- Be professional in your appearance; it communicates respect for yourself and your school.
- Be respectful and professional in all communication.
- Be a smiling, positive presence in the building.
- Do what you're supposed to do when you're supposed to do it, whether or not you want to.

- Keep them informed, especially if they might hear about it elsewhere.
- Encourage them, as they need it too!
- Represent them well when visitors are in the building.
- Be on time.
- Find subs when you are out, and leave quality lesson plans for them to follow.
- Don't give them problems to deal with. Again, handle your own things, as much as you possibly can.
- Don't complain to them, and don't complain about them. Be respectful toward them and their authority at all costs, even if there are some things with which you do not agree.
- When they visit your classroom, make them feel welcome by smiling or nodding.
- Do not overload them with questions. Use your own problem-solving skills, much like you teach your students.
- Thank them appropriately, especially when they offer you some sort of support, or when you are given luncheons, or jeans passes, or whatever the acknowledgment may be.

Administrators want the same things as you do; they want what is best for the students. One honest administrator I interviewed for this book said, "I will have your back all day if you show up every day giving your best, applying proper teaching methodology, and treating students well in the process." Keep this in mind when building relationships with your administrators, and you will gain the support of the senior staff.

Last, but not least, we turn to our relationships with our fellow teachers.

Colleagues

The last relationship we will discuss is the one between you and your colleagues. This relationship is important because your colleagues represent the backbone of your support. They get what it's like to walk daily in the shoes of a teacher in ways that students, parents, and some administrators don't. They are your greatest resource for support and encouragement. Here are the best tips I know for creating great relationships with colleagues:

Think T.E.A.M. The name of this game is teamwork. For those who work together on a grade level team, you will want to work synergistically to achieve better results. For example, this might mean dividing up the lesson planning or dividing up who gathers what materials for a particular unit. It is important that the spirit be one of collaboration, not competition. You are all in this together for a common goal, which is student success. So keep that at the forefront of your mind as you collaborate. Alternatively, some of you may prefer to work alone (I get that), or you may be the only teacher in your building for your particular subject. I would encourage you to be open to possibilities, and then settle into the working style that is best for you.

Get Personal. In addition to curriculum collaboration, you are going to want to establish positive personal relationships with your colleagues at whatever level you are comfortable. I would recommend it not be about school business all of the time. Take time to get to know one another, and be there to support each other when life gets hard. I don't know what I would have done without my teaching buddy next door to me when I was going through a major life crisis. She knew what was going on, and all I had to do was give her a certain look through her classroom door and she would know that I needed her to watch my class for a second while I got myself together.

I cannot emphasize enough the importance of establishing friendships with your colleagues.

Support. Only your fellow teachers truly understand the pressure and complications that may come up in any given day. Support each other. Be there for each other. Do not complain—support. There is a big difference. Listen to each other and offer encouragement and understanding. You are all in this together, and together you can all make it to the finish line.

Build Them Up. I highly encourage you to make encouragement a habit. Build each other up. Shine a light on other people. Comment upon the things you notice about them and about what they bring to the school or teaching experience. This is a habit you can develop if you set the intention and work together with mentors for their support and reminders. Give honest and sincere acknowledgment to people with good ideas and qualities. Never hold back compliments. We all need them! And never hold back a thank you. Be sure to acknowledge and thank your colleagues appropriately for anything that they help with or contribute towards.

Brag on Others. In meetings, go out of your way to recognize and put the spotlight on the accomplishments of teachers you think are doing a great job. Even talk behind their back right in front of their face! You can never go wrong with genuine and sincere praise.

Stay out of the Muck. Gossiping and complaining is the wrong road for you to be on. This might be a difficult one to fight, but you can do it if you're committed. For me, this meant that at some schools, I ate in my classroom instead of in the teachers' lounge. It also has meant that I might not sit near certain people at faculty meetings. Be careful, be aware, and stay guarded. You can't control other people's choices, but you can control your own. Decide that you want to be a person of trust and integrity, and you will find that you will become a valued and admired colleague to work with, and the administrators will know that you are someone they can trust.

Smile! This is a little known secret weapon, and the world needs more of it. Give genuine and positive energy to everyone you pass by in your day through a simple smile.

Remember the Golden Rule. I am sure you know the age-old adage, "Treat people how you want to be treated, even if they don't treat you the same." You may not see eye to eye with everyone, but you can still be respectful and polite. By doing so, you create a safe space for a potential relationship that can one day exist for them, even if it's uncomfortable for you in the moment. One day, you may find them coming to you to bare their soul, and then you'll have a new understanding about them.

This has happened to me countless times. There were teachers who seemed so hard and angry on the outside, who eventually came to me for solace. They knew that I accepted them the way they were and that their stories would be safe with me. I have even had administrators confide in me with problems they were experiencing. The keys are to never judge, and never compromise their trust in you by gossiping. Always maintain a positive regard for everyone. You never know what is going on in their lives.

Through working together and coming from a place of collaboration and support, you can have great relationships with your colleagues and even make friendships that last a lifetime!

Keep Your Relationships Wheel-Rounded

I hope you have seen and now understand the importance of relationships. As a teacher, relationships will encircle everything that happens over the course of your career.

To put this knowledge into a picture, imagine your school relationships as a perfect wheel, with each relationship as one of four equal parts. The wheel cannot function if it is not perfectly round. For each part to maintain its integrity, it must be nurtured. It is your responsibility as a teacher to ensure that you are addressing each part of the wheel appropriately in order for it to move smoothly, the way it was intended.

If you tend to students and not to the parents, your wheel will be bumpy. If you nurture your relationships with your colleagues over your students, you will be off balance. You cannot just choose to focus on one relationship, as they are all important. In fact, if you ruin one, you could ruin others. I have seen instances where the teacher ignored a parent concern (bump), the parent went to admin (bump), the admin reprimanded the teacher (bump), and the teacher felt angry and took it out on the students (bump and collapse). That is definitely a broken wheel!

Remember, a successful teaching career focuses on every relationship, not just one. All of these relationships work together, so be sure to equally cultivate them. They are all synchronistic, and they all operate in harmony with one another. If you build a strong relationship wheel, you will ride upon an easier path and will more quickly accomplish your goals. Most importantly, you will create more *joy*, find more *support*, and make a bigger *impact* along the way, which is every teacher's dream!

stress management

Truth #5: There Will Be Days When You Feel Like It's Too Much

People rarely succeed unless they have fun in what they are doing.
—Dale Carnegie

One of my favorite things about being a teacher is the amount of excitement and variety that we experience each day. However, when I drive home after school, I am always in awe of the amount of energy all of that excitement and variety requires. If you have not yet begun your teaching career, you will see that the pace of a typical school day is fast, and that quite a bit is packed into each moment. This means that there are lots of opportunities for a bad day to get better or for a great day to turn sour. Either way, prepare for a year-long journey and adventure that will challenge every part of who you are. The school year will thrill you, and sometimes it will make you wonder if you're going to survive.

There is a picture of an owl from an unknown source found on the Internet depicting the wisdom and truth behind a typical teacher's experience in any given year. Here is our rendition of that owl's expression:

Teacher on the
first day of school

Teacher on the
last day of school

The truth is, we will all have hard days, and we will all experience times that make us feel like it's just too much. I want you to know that this is normal, and you are going to be okay, largely because you are reading this book and hopefully establishing a firm foundation around the principles put forth. Unfortunately, many teachers who came before you were not given such tools. They did not know what to do with their stress and permanently left the profession, causing students to lose some really great teachers. The condition that so often leads to departure is commonly described as "teacher burnout."

What Is Burnout?

What comes to mind when you hear the term *burnout*? Here's how *Webster's Dictionary* defines burnout: "Exhaustion of physical or emotional strength or motivation usually as a result of prolonged stress or frustration, or a person suffering from burnout." And the sample sentence they provide actually includes a teacher: "Teaching can be very stressful, and many teachers eventually suffer burnout."

Sadly, most teachers experience some type of burnout in their career. According to *TheJournal.com*,[6] teaching "has the highest burnout rate of any public service job." This has to change.

Research finds that in the first five years of teaching, nearly 50 percent of teachers leave the profession. If burnout happens later, the tendency is to either figure out how to overcome it and thrive or just to live with it, essentially *hanging in there*, and likely becoming that infamous teacher that every student and parent hopes not to get and every administrator hopes to not have to deal with.

Do you recall having a teacher who seemed like teaching was the last thing he or she wanted to do? I imagine that when they decided to become a teacher, they did not want to be *that* teacher. They may not even be aware that they've become *that* teacher. They just experienced a slow fall, and didn't know how to get back up. Eventually they became a sad "I don't want to be here" kind of teacher.

When the condition has progressed to that stage, obvious to the students, we call it Loud Burning, Stage 3B. But did you know that most burnout happens unbeknownst to the people around the teacher (Quiet Burning, Stage 3A)? I have seen this time and time again. The teacher suddenly quits halfway through the school year, and everyone has question marks over their heads: *What? Was it that bad? Why didn't she ask for help?*

---

6   https://thejournal.com/articles/2011/11/03/teacher-burnout.aspx

One year, the teacher two doors down from me quit with only one month to go. No one could understand this, especially her students. What exactly happened? How can you make sure you are never in the same situation?

There is hope. This can be avoided. The goal is to make sure you are equipped with awareness, knowledge, and strategies for winning. You will see that there are predictable stages that lead to burnout—let's make sure you can see them coming and that you are ready to immediately act if you start to feel like you are going under water.

To begin with, it's important to understand why teachers get to the point where they feel like their only option is to give up their lifelong dream of being a teacher, and then quit.

Why Does It Happen?

When teachers leave the profession, some of them speak up to explain why they left, but many do not. Many feel shame and embarrassment for quitting, especially if it was in the middle of the school year, so it is difficult to find people willing to be honest about this somewhat taboo topic.

However, some do talk. According to our research and anonymous interviews with teachers who have quit (or want to quit), here are some common examples of reasons they cite for walking out the door:

Too Stressful

"I'm in my first year of teaching, and even though I love teaching, I have never been so stressed. There is so much pressure to constantly improve your practice that every time I feel like I'm getting on top of something (planning, grading, etc.), something new is thrown at me. I want to be the best I can, but it's only now I'm realizing that as a teacher, you can never relax. I'm not sure I can do this."

Feelings of Isolation

"I felt so alone. I knew I needed help but didn't know who could provide it. I couldn't ask the other teachers for help because they were busy with their own stuff. I didn't want to ask my mentor for help because that might look like weakness, and what if my mentor reported everything to the principal? Who could I turn to? Finally, I just gave up."

Testing Pressure

"I am really getting tired of this. Why is there so much focus on test scores? And why so much pressure on us as teachers? My pressure gets placed on the students, and that is not fair to them. I am spending weeks and weeks' worth of instructional time either practicing or administering mandated testing. No wonder they hate school. That is not teaching, and that is not what is best for students! Even worse, they defend the continual testing by claiming that we 'use the data to drive instruction.' Oh, really? Ha, I better not talk about that one."

Mental and Physical Exhaustion

"I did not realize I would be spending every evening and weekend working on school things. It's too much. I never feel done! I feel like there is an endless list of things to do, and students and parents are constantly demanding mental energy. Physically, I'm spent as well.

Starting very early in the morning, I am on my feet the entire day teaching or speed walking up and down the hallways and stairs a million times. It's exhausting!"

Lack of Support

"I felt attacked and judged, not supported. I felt like parents were blaming me, and the administrators were taking the parents' side. When did everything become the teacher's fault? It surely wasn't that way when I was a student. If teachers cannot get support within their own school, then why bother? Why would I want to go to work? And then I hear teacher-bashing in the press, and it makes me ashamed to be one. I'm a good person and a hard worker. I'm not going to spend the rest of my life feeling like I have to defend myself and prove myself."

Not Feeling Good Enough

"I felt guilty because there were so many needs, and I couldn't meet them all. Sometimes I'd have no idea how to help a student, and it made me feel like a bad teacher. I saw all of these other teachers getting all of the attention from administration, so I just figured I'm not good enough to do this."

Student Behavior

"I couldn't deal with the behavior issues. I mean, what is up with kids these days? It's like they have no respect for authority. I even had a student roll their eyes at me and tell me they 'don't need to listen to me, b****.' I would be insane to put up with that."

No Work-Life Balance

"I had no personal life as a teacher. All I did was go to school, come home, grade papers, or work on lesson plans. Then it was sleep, wake up, repeat. I lost all of my hobbies and all of my friends because I was too tired to go out. Even though I was newly married, my husband knew that we couldn't start planning a family while I was teaching because I couldn't imagine attempting to raise a child on top of everything else. It's amazing our marriage lasted."

It is sad to hear these expressions of despair and frustration. Even though I've felt some version of each one of these, I promise, *it doesn't have to be that way. There is a better way of doing things. You can love your life as a teacher.*

Although specific reasons may be given as to why teachers leave, my experience is that it is more than one thing that leads to quitting. It is a piling up of many reasons, and it is the negligence in addressing those reasons that leads people to the end. I speak with passion on this topic because I have been through the many phases of burnout. In fact, I have felt like a passenger on the rollercoaster named Burnout, having lived through every turn on the ride. I know what it's like to come home and wonder if I made the right choice in becoming a teacher. I know what it's like to cry and wonder if anything I am doing is making a single difference for anyone. And I know what it's like to struggle with the pressure of feeling like there's no option except quitting but feeling like I'll fail myself and my students if I do.

My number one hope in writing this book is to help good teachers remain in teaching. I want this book to make teachers feel understood and supported, and initiate conversations around topics

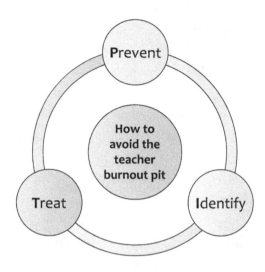

hidden for too long. The teacher burnout problem needs a voice and a solution. I also want teachers to know that if they absolutely feel like there is no other alternative but to leave, that they can do it with their head held high.

But I'm going to guess that teaching is your calling, and you know that in your soul. Even if it feels unstable at times, you can persevere and come out on top. You can learn to accept the bumps, navigate around them with ease, and successfully enjoy the ride. While it took me many years to figure out how to avoid looking like that "end of the year owl," you can be spared. If you follow this prescription, it is with utmost confidence that I say you will *not* be that bedraggled owl at the end of the year; you will finish looking just as good as when you started.

Solution

Your biggest weapon is going to be maintaining an awareness of the warning signs, and then treating burnout like you would a cold. First with some TLC, and then with more aggressive tactics as needed.

Prevent. Identify. Treat.

The best defense is a great offense, so the best way to avoid the pit of burnout is to stay on its perimeter.

Prevent it from happening

Identify the stage

Treat it with solutions

Prevent

Benjamin Franklin once said, "An ounce of prevention is worth a pound of cure." As a preventive measure, be sure to do these things:

1. Apply the principles in this book.

   I wrote this entire book in order to prevent teacher burnout. The good news is that the simple fact you are reading this book significantly lessens your risk of burnout. Through these pages, you have been offered tried-and-true resources and principles geared towards helping you avoid even the potential for burnout. Burnout does not happen overnight; it is like a kettle of water coming to a boiling point. It takes time, and will eventually get so hot that it can boil over. Applying the tools in this book will help keep you from reaching this catastrophic point in your life. I further encourage you to revisit these principles every summer before you start school, and keep them close as you ride out the year.

2. Find a mentor.

   Doing anything on our own is a hard way to learn. Having someone who's a decade or two ahead of you and can point out the pitfalls and shortcuts of teaching can take years off of your learning curve and help you avoid many frustrations altogether.

Mentoring is a concept in the education system that isn't always actively practiced, so the idea of approaching other teachers and asking if they'd be willing to give you the benefit of their decades of experience and wisdom may seem out of left field, but that doesn't mean you shouldn't seek someone out. Even if it's the first time they've been asked, I'm sure they'd be both honored and flattered.

What I hope is that this method of passing on wisdom and experience becomes standard practice, as it is immensely helpful. I also hope that schools implement more mentor programs where older students help younger ones in developing an appreciation for the gifts of leadership and how good it feels to give back.

Ideally, your school district or principal will have a mentor arranged for you. However, since this doesn't always happen, you might need to take some initiative. If you're not assigned one, the first place to look is the room next-door. Our greatest resources often are in the classrooms right next to us or just down the hall. Don't be afraid or ashamed to ask for help. They have been in your shoes. The wonderful thing about our fellow teachers is that we understand each other, and there is no substitute for someone who truly gets it.

We all need support. We all need to feel understood. We all can benefit from mentorship from those with more experience than we have—we just need to raise our hand and ask. You are not a failure if you ask for help. It's okay.

You are well on your way to a great year if you have completed these two steps. However, times may get rough and you might wonder what is going on and if you should be worried. Let's investigate the next part of staying on the perimeter of the burnout pit: How to identify and treat the beast.

Identify and Treat

The truth is that burnout does not happen suddenly. It is a process. Like many things, if identified and treated early, it is fully curable. It is my belief that there are four very clear stages that one goes through before the end of the line:

1. Overwhelmed
2. Exhausted
3. Burning
4. Done

The problem is that if we do not treat our symptoms early, they will lead to our worst fear.

With nearly 50 percent of teachers reaching Stage 4 in five years or less, we need a better form of treatment and prevention. Let's examine each stage and see how each one is treated or cured.

Stage 1: Overwhelmed

As a new teacher, you can plop yourself right into Stage 1. This is where you will exist for most of the year. It is okay to feel overwhelmed! And there is nothing wrong with you. You are still loved, and there are lots of ways to make it better and easier.

The good news is that Stage 1 is the most treatable. It requires keeping the right mindset as found in Truth #1 and embracing procedural and time-saving strategies like those found in Truth #2 and Truth #3. Even though starting a new job is exciting, it is still stressful. You know you can do it, and your excitement and energy may stay high. Yet, it is still a lot, and it feels overwhelming. That is normal. You might hang out in Stage 1 for quite a while, and if so, that would be a huge success. In fact, if you create a teaching life for yourself that never goes beyond this stage, you really are a superhero!

While you may still have lots of energy in this stage, be careful not to push too hard just because you have extra energy and enthusiasm. Our bodies and minds can only handle a high level of stress for so long. If left untreated, feeling overwhelmed will definitely lead to Stage 2.

Stage 2: Exhausted

This is a familiar feeling for many teachers, so do not be surprised or upset if you find yourself here. It is normal, you are okay, and you will get through this. In this stage, your energy and enthusiasm have faded. You are tired, and you may even feel depressed. But like Stage 1, it is also curable if you don't ignore it.

Exhaustion is your body's way of telling you it's time to stop and make some changes. If you don't, your mind and spirit get heavy, your immune system weakens, you feel sick and/or extremely tired, and you may end up in bed for a few days, or even worse. If you find yourself in this place, it's time to rest.

Don't take this stage lightly. It could turn into disaster. The good news is that this is not difficult to treat, but you *must* treat it. You must give yourself permission to regroup and focus on your health and well-being.

For example, examine your recent sleep habits. Have you been sleeping enough? You may only need a good, single, solid night's sleep to rejuvenate your energy. Sometimes a weekend can do the trick, or maybe a long break. If that is not it, maybe you should take a day off to check in with your doctor, get rest, make plans for changes in your classroom, or catch up on home business. Sometimes if our school world gets crazy, so does our home world. Don't be afraid to use your personal days for personal care. It's okay! Your students will appreciate that you took some time to rejuvenate.

While you are taking the time to stop, rest, and regroup, be sure to identify the source of your exhaustion, if possible. If the exhaustion is from overload and feeling overworked, you may want to go back to Truth #3 and make some adjustments. Also, pay close attention to the next Truth about self-care, as this will need to be at the forefront of your mind moving forward. Reversal is possible at this stage, as long as you recognize it early and treat it right away. If you don't, it could become clinical, and lead to Stage 3, a place where you never want to find yourself.

Stage 3: Burning

If you were a student in this stage, you would be labeled "At Risk: In Danger of Failing." If feeling overwhelmed and being exhausted are left unaddressed, you will most likely end up here, and you may feel frustrated, confused, and depressed. It gets complicated and messy at this stage, especially because it could look different for everyone. For example, it can be a slow fade, or it can seem to happen quickly. It can be quiet or loud. Let's examine the difference:

A. Quiet Burning: Only you know about it.

It festers inside, it eats you up, but to the outside school world, nothing appears to be wrong. That is, until you are suddenly out "sick" for days and weeks.

The danger with Quiet Burning is in its progression. Like most things, it starts in the mind and then can quickly manifest into behaviors. Due to this, your best defense is to become very aware of your thinking so that you can recognize it and reverse it.

When it happened to me, I knew that my thoughts were negative and not healthy, but it took me a while to learn a strategy to correct it. Later, I will be sharing this strategy so you can use it in case you ever find yourself in this unfortunate and lonely place.

B. Loud Burning: Everyone around you knows it.

This is dangerous and toxic. You might be unaware of how Loud Burning is consuming your being, or you might be aware but in denial, or perhaps you have decided not to care anymore. Here are some examples of what it may look like on the outside to other people. They will see a teacher who

- Complains *a lot*.
- Is absent more often, or is always late, and it doesn't faze them.
- Looks exhausted and seems to care less about appearance.
- "Wings" their lessons instead of planning them, or plans the easiest thing *for themselves.*
- Is always counting down to the end of the day, to Friday, to the next break, etc.
- May be found sitting a lot; teaches from behind their desk.
- Yells or speaks negatively to their class and puts them down.
- Ignores the students.
- Cultivates messiness: clutters their classroom and workspace areas.
- Does not respond to email or does so with abrasion and unprofessionalism.

- Has continual problems with students, parents, and administrators.
- Is always negative in words and facial expressions.
- Mocks other people, even their own students.
- Pushes back on everything and complains during meetings.
- Always seems frustrated, annoyed, and unhappy.

You don't want to be here! This stage is unproductive, unhealthy, unpredictable, and unstable. This stage requires immediate intervention. Again, do not stay here! *Find a great sub to take care of your students, and get out of this stage as fast as you can!* You know this is the right thing to do. The students deserve better, and you deserve better than to accept this as your normal.

Again, you must not stay here! Are you hearing the fire alarm yet? Immediately reverse this or you will rapidly proceed to Stage 4. We do not want this type of teacher in front of our students.

Be sure to reread and apply all treatments from Stages 1 and 2. Do you still have a mentor? It would be extremely important that you find someone to talk to about how you feel, even if it's a therapist or life coach. Remember, you do not need to do this alone. Because this stage is the riskiest place to find yourself, the rest of the chapter (following the Stage 4 description) will focus on additional strategies to help you recover.

Stage 4: Done

If Stage 3 goes untreated, you will find that you cannot go on anymore; you are done.

Burnt. Cooked. Toasted. Fried.

This is the worst place to find yourself because a reversal, though perhaps possible, is extremely difficult and unlikely. This is where you feel beat down by everything. Scars are forming, resentment and blame dominate your being, and you just need to get out. You quit. You resign. You can't go to school for even one more day. You might call in sick, or you might not bother to call. You are d-o-n-e.

Sometimes this occurs more conveniently between school years, but not all the time. Tragically, almost *10 percent* of new teachers do not make it through their first year. It is worse in the UK, where *40 percent* do not make it! This means they leave during the instructional year, causing all sorts of problems.

When teachers suddenly quit like that, it is because they have entered this stage. All of the other stages were there, but no interventions took place. It could have gone unnoticed by everyone around the teacher. They leave the career they paid and trained for, and they leave precious students wondering what happened. And it's all because the other stages went untreated.

So let's back up a little and make sure you are loaded up with treatment options. In addition to speaking with a mentor and applying every intervention as described in Stages 1 and 2, if you ever find yourself burning in Stage 3, here are a few extra adjustments you might consider.

- *Make a change.* Change your grade level, change your topic, or change your school. I taught the same grade level for 12 years and didn't realize what I missed until I decided to get trained in another specialty. It was adventurous and fresh to try something new! Please do not allow yourself to slip into Stage 4 if you have only experienced one thing or one school. Every position is different, and every school is different. I promise, there is great hope to be found in change.

- *Look outward.* Help someone. Pick one student and make an intentional difference. Sometimes when I felt depressed, it was because I didn't believe I was making a difference. I was treating my class like one big unit instead of as a canvas made up of beautiful individual masterpieces. When I decided to hyperfocus on them as individuals, everything changed. I began to choose one or two students each day, and I would intentionally pay extra attention to their needs. This always worked to cure my feelings of uselessness and bring back my excitement for teaching again.

- *Become present.* Being mindful of the present moment is a gift we can instantly give ourselves. A lot of stress comes from thinking about the past or thinking about the future. Try being in the present, the moment *right now*. Notice your breathing, become aware of yourself and your surroundings, and just … be at peace. Not only will this practice make you feel better, it is what our students require for them to feel like they matter.

- *Find joy in the students.* Remember, they are the reason we teach. Sometimes it is hard with everything going on to remember to find our joy through them. While curriculum comes and goes, and school initiatives are often fleeting and passing waves, this one thing stays the same. You may have lost your joy for the long list of to-dos you may have, but find your joy in the students. It is there if you intentionally look for it. We just have to remember to look.

- *Mind strategy.* Do a "Thinking 180." Sometimes, our minds can be mean to us. I have caught myself thinking some terribly negative thoughts, and never knew what to do with them besides feeling shame. One day I challenged myself. I told myself I would catch a negative thought in the air the second it came out and replace it with a positive one.

"How much longer is this meeting? It is such a waste of time!" became, *"I am honored to be part of a staff that meets together and works toward common goals for the good of the children."*

"This paperwork is insane" became, *"I can do this. It won't take too long."*

The more I practiced doing a 180 in my thinking, the more natural it became. Now it automatically happens. My brain automatically sees the good in almost every situation, and this can happen for you, too. It takes work, but it is possible to switch your thinking. In doing so, you will experience a wonderful shift in your energy and state of mind. Let's see how Amy did this...

Case Study: Amy

Meet Amy. She is in her third year of teaching, and she is starting to doubt her choice of profession. She loves teaching but is having trouble with all of the "other stuff." Lately, she knows that she has lost her enthusiasm and prays that her students don't know that she is crying on the inside. With all of her strength, she is still forcing herself to be an outstanding teacher for them, but privately, she is ashamed of her thoughts. Like many in Quiet Burning, she is put together on the outside, but it is a different story in her head. She is now driving home from school, frustrated. Her insides are confused and screaming for help. Let's step inside Amy's mind to see what's going on:

I can't do this anymore.
Why am I doing this to myself?
I don't deserve this.

This is insane.
This isn't what I signed up for.
These kids don't want to learn.

When is the next break?
How many days until summer?

No one appreciates me.
I am replaceable.
I want to quit.

No one can know what I'm thinking.

I am not paid enough for this!
I'm tired of interacting with hundreds
of humans every day.
No one understands what we do!

My plate is full. In fact, it is breaking
and dumping out all over the place.

I'm trapped.
There's nothing left in me to give.
I can't get a grip.

I'm exhausted.
I'm exhausted.
I'm exhausted...

Amy comes home from school and cries on her bed. She frantically searches the Internet for help where she finds and downloads a book called *Teacher's Field Guide*. She reads it cover to cover. Immediately, she realizes that because she ignored the feeling of being overwhelmed and exhausted, she is in Stage 3A, Quiet Burning. She decides to utilize a personal day to stay home and make a plan to apply the interventions that she missed in Stages 1 and 2 (taking care of herself, lightening her load, reminding herself of the bigger picture, checking her relationships, etc.), and then she does a Thinking 180 exercise. She writes down all of her negative thoughts and reverses the thought pattern.

Thinking 180: Amy

Current Thought/ Feeling/Reaction	180
I can't do this anymore.	I can't do this on my own, but I'm going to find the right support to get me through.
I don't deserve this.	I deserve whatever I allow and what I don't address. Will I continue to allow this, or do I need to address it?
This is insane.	The most important person to be in control when things feel like they're not is me. I'll take this minute by minute until I'm through it and then ask myself how I got in it.
This isn't what I signed up for.	This isn't what I expected. Were my expectations off, or have things changed? Will I adjust, or do I need to speak with someone about my role?

These kids don't want to learn.	My students aren't responding to this subject or style of learning. Who can I talk to who can suggest some ideas they've seen work? Am I creating what they are craving? A safe, loving, inspiring environment?
When is the next break? How many days until summer?	I was blessed with the gift of teaching and I only have so many days in the lives of my students. I will cherish every day as an opportunity to share that gift in a way that makes a meaningful difference.
No one appreciates me.	Every day I take time to validate one genuine and special thing about myself, a student, and another teacher. The thing I appreciate most about myself is that I take time to care.
I am replaceable.	I see the unique gifts in every single one of my students, the other teachers, and the staff here in the school. We are the only group exactly like us, and I'm the only one who can add my particular gifts and flavor to this incredible mix.
I want to quit.	Today I feel like my unique gifts aren't making a difference, and I am exhausted. I will take steps to address it.
No one can know what I'm thinking.	I will not be ashamed. I am human, and it is okay that I am tired.
I am not paid enough for this.	This was never about the money, but today I need to look at my vision from Truth #1 and notes of appreciation to remind me of my purpose.

I'm tired of interacting with hundreds of humans every day.	I love what I do, but if I ever find I need to take a personal day to re-center, I'll take one.
No one understands what we do.	I will honor my unique expertise and do my best to be understanding with those who haven't had the advantage of my experience.
My plate is full. In fact, it is breaking and dumping out all over the place.	I'm never in this alone. If it feels like too much, I'll talk to my mentor/coach or reach out for community.
I'm trapped.	I chose to teach because it's what I was born to do, and if I can do this well, I can do anything. Every industry is in need of people with the valuable skill set I was born with.
There's nothing left in me to give.	In order to have something to give I need to take time to receive. I will take exceptional care of myself and take the recommendations laid out in this book.
I can't get a grip.	In my class, we will be respectful of anyone who needs to take a moment. We will have a sign that anyone can use if they need a two-minute time out, even if the one who needs it is me.
I'm exhausted.	To be my best I need to take care of myself first. If I find I'm getting behind, I commit to taking better care of myself.

Amy is left feeling excited and positive, and she is encouraged and refreshed for her next day at school. She went from feeling helpless, to feeling hope through her plan for renewal.

Like Amy, I hope that if you ever catch yourself in this place, you will reread this book and apply this reverse-thinking technique to help you remember that you are in control of your thoughts. You have the power to turn around negative thinking the moment it shows up in your mind. You also have the ability to make lifestyle and work-related changes that can refresh your teaching journey. *As long as you are willing, there is hope.*

As much as I truly believe that almost all of you will be able to prevent and treat feelings of burnout, what if you are still wondering if teaching was the right choice for you? We would hate to lose anyone who feels like teaching is their life mission, but if you are still questioning things, please feel safe to admit it. It's okay.

Should I Quit?

First of all, do not be ashamed. It is okay. If you decide to leave teaching, it is better to make that decision when you are in a healthy state of mind (not when you are at your lowest point) and after careful consideration and counsel from people you can trust.

But first, ask yourself these important questions:

- Do you remember why you started, and the difference you hoped to make? (Truth #1)
- Is your classroom management plan working? (Truth #2)
- Are you giving attention to how you can lighten your workload and have a healthy work-life balance? (Truth #3)

- Are you at peace with the people and relationships in your life? (Truth #4)
- Have you implemented any strategies for burnout? (Truth #5)
- Are you taking proper care of yourself? (Truth #6)
- Are you keeping the big picture of life in mind? (Truth #7)

If you can honestly answer yes to those questions, *and* have thought about it while in a healthy state of mind, *and* have received counsel from people you trust, then perhaps it is indeed time for you to leave the profession. This does not mean you are a failure! If you decide to leave, it just means that something else awaits you.

We want devoted and committed teachers to lead our youth. We want the very best to stay and thrive. Our children deserve it, and it would be a disservice to our students and society to stay doing something that you were not made for. It's okay.

The Bottom Line

You matter. Your life is important, and your level of joy in your chosen vocation is important. Choosing to teach is an honorable decision on your part, and I hope that you never have to suffer through the stages of burnout.

If you do start to slip, I hope that the information in this chapter will help you to reverse those feelings and learn to thrive again. If it is recognized and treated early, as outlined in this chapter, burnout is curable. Apply the principles and mindsets in all of these Truths, find a caring mentor, and this might be something that you never have to confront.

Always keep in mind that you will have days that are hard, but there is hope, and you can do this!

You are normal.

You are okay.

You are not alone.

self-management

Truth #6: Self-Care Is Not Selfish

You cannot serve from an empty vessel.
—Eleanor Brownn

teachers, like most parents, are natural givers. This can lead to enormous strains on both your personal and professional life. You have the great responsibility to be in your classroom early and ready to go, and then you must maintain focus, interaction, and excitement throughout the day. Couple that with the multitudes of students for which you are responsible, and you can imagine most days aren't simply a walk in the park.

One thing I've noticed in my two decades of teaching is that teachers can easily get so busy taking care of other people that they neglect themselves. I cannot tell you how many times I've had to tell my coughing, sneezing, tired colleagues to take a sick day. "I'll be fine," they say, and then they wear themselves out from giving more than they have.

What they believe to be a selfless and strong work ethic is actually quite the opposite. It isn't a good idea to show up to work sick. It exposes everyone to the germs, and it is hard to stay upbeat when you feel down. It isn't helping you, or anyone else, to pretend that you are fine when you really are completely exhausted and need a break. It says to the world, "I do not respect myself enough to take care of myself." If you don't hear anything else in this entire book, please hear this: *Taking care of yourself is a sign of self-respect, and it is a loving gift to those who interact with you.*

The Greatest Gift You Can Give Your Students

The best thing we can do for the people we serve is to take good care of ourselves. Corporate America knows this. As I was studying to become a teacher, I was a corporate health and exercise specialist working in major corporations like PepsiCo, Xerox, and Becton Dickinson helping them keep their employees healthy. These companies, and many more like them, understand the value of a healthy employee. Some of the benefits include:

- Increased productivity
- Increased morale
- Increased mental and physical energy
- Decreased absenteeism
- Decreased sickness
- Decreased stress

I encouraged healthy habits within the company, including nutrition counseling, teaching group exercise classes, administering formal fitness and body composition tests, and sending out informational publications.

I also enjoyed giving lectures and seminars to the corporate employees on areas related to health and wellness.

In the weeks following one of my wellness seminars, an employee approached me and stated that something I had said really stuck with him and even motivated him to start exercising. He told me that the week of my seminar, he had just bought a new car and was spending a lot of time making sure it remained clean. The hardest habit for him to kick was not eating potato chips and french fries in his car. I didn't know him or his story at the seminar, but apparently I said, "Look at how we treat our shiny new cars compared to how we treat our bodies. Why is that? We need to start treating ourselves with the same respect we would a shiny new car." For him, that was all he needed to get moving towards a healthier lifestyle. It was a decision he made, and then the rest followed. From that point on, whenever he would pass me on his way to a workout, he would say, "Shiny new car!" In making an intentional lifestyle change, his focus and energy improved, and he said he'd never been happier.

Far too often teachers forget how important their own health and well-being actually is. It is only after they feel burned out, tired, and overworked that they might acknowledge it is time for a change. Personal health is commonly a slow and sometimes quiet decline. It could take months, if not years, of overdedication to the job at the expense of personal needs before one realizes that it went too far. To that end, this Truth tells us that it is *not* selfish to focus on self-care.

Anyone who has had some sort of surgery, or even the flu, knows what it feels like to be unable to move for days. What good are we in this world if our health starts to slip? If any part of our body, mind, or spirit starts to weaken, we start to weaken. This chapter is dedicated to helping you take care of yourself, because you matter. Your health, your well-being, and your happiness are directly related to the results you can expect in life.

When we are healthier, we feel happier. A healthy, happy teacher is the only one who can create a healthy, happy classroom.

This practice starts with giving yourself permission to focus on *you*. Remember? This is not being selfish; it is actually the most loving and giving thing you can do for those who interact with you. The best version of you will create the best results for both you and those around you. Which teacher do you aspire to be: the one who wears themselves out from giving more than they have and ends up in a stage of burnout, or the one who monitors themselves and takes care of themselves to ensure they can be at their best for their students?

Because this is a service profession, you must position yourself accordingly. Following are the best strategies I know to help you show up every day with a smile on your face, eager to serve, and representing the best, most energetic version of yourself.

Let's start by ensuring your *give meter* is resoundingly full:

Tip #1: Monitor the Give Meter

We only have so much capacity to give. Think about it: If I asked you for a banana, you couldn't give me one if you didn't have one. This applies to energy as well. You can't give what you don't have. In order to have enough to give, you must be at a place as an individual where you can overflow for your students and for those in your life. This must be a decision you make and a commitment you make to yourself. In order to have an overflow, you must regularly recharge your *give meter*. Once it gets poured out, it must be refilled.

If there is not a strategy in place to refresh yourself, you will feel constantly drained.

To refresh yourself, try to think of things to do that feed your energy. How many times have you felt a sense of euphoria after a great workout? Or extra energy after a healthy meal? Or truly alive after a great social outing with friends? Or refreshed after a short nap? You probably felt reinvigorated in those moments. But teachers still struggle with this because they are givers at heart.

It's easy to trick ourselves into thinking that if we stay late at school and spend most of our free time grading papers or working on lesson plans, that we are being a good teacher. That is a lie. Good teachers take care of themselves so that they are able to give to others.

Your *give meter* should always remain full, ready for you to dip into it when needed. Perhaps you have a student going through a difficult time, or one that cannot seem to fit in, or one having a tough time learning a new concept or lesson. It is in those moments that your students need for you to be alert, connected, and physically capable of giving it your all. But, if you are down on yourself, and exhausted or unhealthy, it will show in how you interact with your students. Always strive to keep it full, and the tips that follow will help you do just that.

Tip #2: Leave 10 Percent in Reserve for You

While we want to go into each day with our *give meter* on full, we have to be careful to make sure it doesn't get completely depleted by the evening. One of the best ways to ensure you don't run dry by the end of the day is to keep some reserve in the tank. Most people are wired to give 10 percent more than they have. But I want you to take a different approach and consider always retaining 10 percent of what you have to give. This behavior will make certain there is always something left in the well *for you* or for unexpected situations that come up.

It takes courage to make sure you leave room for this every day. But again, the gift of self-care is the best thing you can do for everyone. You never know when a situation might arise that calls for that last little bit. There may be a moment when you least expect it in life, or in the classroom, to give a superhuman effort. If you've been overextending yourself day after day and feel tapped out, when the time comes for you to be heroic, you will sputter and slump.

Ten percent for you, every day. Try to commit to that. More than anything else, this is what you need to see as your sacred gift to yourself. That may mean not staying at school until the late hours of the evening, not joining committees or volunteering to coach, or not volunteering to tutor extra students after school if it means you aren't left with your 10 percent. It means that you are a real example of living life on healthy terms while looking for opportunities to make a real difference in ways you uniquely can that matter most. It doesn't mean you are only doing the job halfway; it is actually quite the opposite. This is especially true when you first begin your career. Don't let being new make you feel like you have to prove that you're a team player by taking on more than your main assignment. You will have plenty of time in your career to take on extra things. At the beginning, it's all about you.

Tip #3: The Sleep Factor—Go to Bed

One of the best ways to stay refreshed is to make sure you always get a good night's sleep. I have found this to be the most important thing for me. I call this "The Sleep Factor." How much is enough? The National Sleep Foundation tells us that adults need seven to nine hours per night. Personally, I am at my best with eight to nine hours of sleep. If I do not get a proper night's sleep, getting out of bed feels like a chore. Teaching feels extremely hard and demanding. The kids irritate me more, and I am more inclined to look at the clock all day waiting for dismissal.

Because I know this about myself, it is my priority every night to shut it down by 9 p.m. on school nights. I know that may sound outrageous to some of you, but for me, it is what I discipline myself to do. As a result, I wake up many mornings before the alarm goes off, excited to get out of bed and start the day. I also find that I am more pleasant to be around, and I am stronger for my students.

"The Sleep Factor" directly affects my ability to enter into the day with a positive attitude and the energy needed for a fantastic school day. It also helps me be punctual. The same may or may not be true for you. But human physiology will tell you that everyone needs sleep. It is right up there with oxygen, water, and food. You just cannot exist without it. As teachers, we have early mornings all of the time that require us to be awake and at our optimal performance level immediately, so I strongly encourage you to give yourself and your students the gift of proper rest.

Teaching is quite unusual, isn't it? We have to show up for school at an exact time because our "customers" are coming down the hallway into our room, ready or not! We cannot just stroll in a little late. At one district where I worked, we had to fingerprint in every morning, and that data was carefully tracked. Talk about pressure! I have been able to succeed with this one by getting proper sleep and setting the clock 10 minutes ahead in my car, which helps me make sure I'm not going the minimum speed. I know that sounds silly, but it works for me because I have the tendency to drive too slow. Speaking of being in the car…

Tip #4: Use Your Commute Wisely

Fact: The commute is going to happen. It can help us, hurt us, or do nothing. Why not use it to help? Every morning on our drive to school, we have a choice. What are we going to listen to and/or think about? I want to encourage you to use your commute intentionally. I believe that what I do in the car on the way to school significantly impacts my day. Make this time valuable, and always leave early to give yourself sufficient margins to arrive at school without feeling flustered or stressed. The worst thing you can do is to constantly feel rushed. I consider my commute almost sacred. Here are four things I do every day, without fail:

- **Pick the Right Frequency.** I make sure that the radio station I have on is positive and uplifting. Otherwise, it's off.
- **Make a List, Check It Twice.** I list things for which I am grateful. Sometimes it's in my head; sometimes it's in a low whisper.
- **Set Expectations.** I set an intention for the day to be "positive, polite, and professional." I actually say those three words either in my head or in a whisper.
- **Smile, Smile, Smile.** Lastly, and this is a requirement that I am really strict on, I force myself to smile. Yes, that's right. In the car, alone, and definitely before I get out of the car, I make myself smile. I call it my *One-Second Smile*.

Anyone who knows me knows that I smile all of the time. I love to smile! It truly is a reflection of the joy I feel inside. But there are mornings when the last thing I feel like doing is smiling. As hard as it might be, even if I am kicking and screaming on the inside while I do it, I still force myself to smile before I get out of the car. It's a discipline I have continued to use because it works. Ninety-nine percent of the time, just that one-second act creates an attitude shift into the positive zone. Go ahead, I dare you to *One-Second Smile* right now and see what happens.

Tip #5: Mentally Prepare for Giving and Decision Making

Yes, we are teachers and it's natural that we go into each day prepared to teach the curriculum. But because this is a *service* and *helping* profession, we don't want to forget to prepare ourselves mentally for the level of giving that occurs daily. Hopefully, you will have refreshed yourself and are ready to walk in with a full tank and a high awareness of your *give meter* because you will spend the rest of the day pouring out energy. It is best to know this and be ready.

You also want to mentally prepare to feel the emotional drain that comes with extensive decision making. Have you ever wondered how many decisions a teacher makes in a single day? Researcher Philip Jackson said that elementary teachers have 200 to 300 exchanges with students every hour (between 1,200 and 1,500 a day), most of which are unplanned and unpredictable, and call for teacher decisions or judgments. That is a lot of thinking!

Decision making requires tremendous mental energy, and that is part of why teaching is so exhausting. You may notice this difference on a teacher workday (a professional day without students) when there is no interaction with students. Those days are typically much less draining. Knowing this ahead of time will help you understand where your exhaustion comes from, and it will hopefully motivate you to step into the day alert and well rested.

Here is an additional tip: To address the enormous number of decisions that have to be made, start each day or each week by closing your eyes and anticipating some of the decisions with which you'll be faced. Visualize the situation, consider your answers, and place them in your mental vocabulary. This visualization exercise will help to reduce the pain and immediate stress a lot of decisions require. You will have already thought it through, and you will be more likely to address situations on the fly with minimal wear and tear.

Tip #6: Exercise: It's Not Just for Summer

Some people exercise regularly out of habit because they have done it their whole lives. Some people force themselves to exercise because they are trying to lose weight or they know it is a good idea to help sustain health. Then, there are those who cringe at the word. Is that you? That's okay—we still love you!

Many days after teaching I feel like I already spent the entire day exercising. Doesn't all of that walking the students to and fro count for anything? Or, how about all of the mental energy I expend. Doesn't that count?

The truth is that it's not about "what counts"; it's about "time out." Take time out for YOU. Time to be in your own space and your own mind, free from distractions, to move your body. Think of an exercise session as your stress management session, where you can disconnect from the regular challenges the day presents and just focus your mind and soul on … well, your mind and soul.

For example, I absolutely love the way my body feels when I exercise. It feels like a mini-vacation to me and helps me think more clearly. There are other added benefits to exercise as well: reduced blood pressure, reduced risk of many diseases, better weight control, elevation in mood, better sleep, and increased energy. Believe it or not, exercise is a great cure for fatigue! Additionally, studies show your body releases endorphins, or feel good chemicals, with just 20 minutes of sustained activity. All of this means reduced stress levels, which is important because stress can wreak havoc in all areas of our lives.

With all of these benefits, why wouldn't we exercise? No time? No energy? I get it. I have used those excuses before. They are normal and we are all human. But, I finally figured out that if I exercise in the morning, I can't use either one of those excuses. I don't have to devote a ton of time, sometimes it is only 10 minutes, but it is enough to get the blood flowing and help me clear my mind and feel prepared for the day ahead.

Exercising after school is also a great option, especially if you are monitoring your tank and have energy left in reserve. To keep you motivated, try joining a group class or going for a walk with a friend or family member. Is there a sport that you loved as a child? Get back into it! I have taken adult figure skating lessons after school and even ended up competing as an adult. My students loved that I was enjoying myself outside of school. It's never too late to have fun! Give yourself permission to enjoy an activity. It doesn't make you less of a teacher. It doesn't mean you are less committed.

There are also in-school options that could work as well. I know of a teacher who would bring her walking shoes to school every day. As soon as the students were dismissed, she would go for a walk around the school grounds. Then, she would return and focus on her paperwork.

Also, at one of the schools where I taught, there was a track around the playground. Teachers would walk laps during recess or on breaks instead of sitting on a bench or remaining in the classroom. I challenge you to find something that works for you, and give it a five-day test! If at the end of five days you are not feeling better, then try a different approach. It doesn't matter how long, when, or how; what matters is you give yourself the gift of time out *for you*.

Tip #7: Choose Healthy Eating

Remember the phrase garbage in, garbage out? What we put into our bodies has tremendous influence on our attitude, energy, and performance. I think that teachers have added challenges in this area.

Here's why:

- We eat at scheduled exact times (i.e., 11:37 a.m.–12:07 p.m.).
- We start the day so early that breakfast is often difficult.
- It is a "snacky" culture. Students bring snacks; the teachers' lounge has snacks.
- Food is used as gifts, rewards, and for celebration.
- We cannot leave the premises for lunch.

These all make it very easy to eat in an unhealthy way. I know there is something alluring about having a cupcake with the students on their birthday, but have you ever calculated how many birthdays are celebrated each school year? One year, I figured out that we had 23 birthday parties in just one year, which averages to more than one every other week. That's a whole lot of cupcakes!

To help in this area, I suggest you have a plan for your eating. For example, consider packing your own lunch, so that you remain in control of the options. Before I invested in a mini-fridge, as mentioned in Truth #3, I would pack a small cooler each day. Both options have worked wonders for me. Over the weekend, I shop for everything I need for the week ahead. This way, I have healthy snacks and lunch items on hand, and I'm not at all inclined to eat the unhealthy snacks or eat cafeteria food.

I also have learned to discipline myself to just say "no" to student sweets and faculty room treats. This was not easy at first, but once I made the decision, it no longer presented itself as an option. It became "no, thank you" quite easily. So much of what we want to do in life lies in simply making the decision, and then practicing discipline. I promise, you can do this!

But overeating or junky eating isn't always the greatest culprit for teachers. I know many teachers who become so busy during the school day that they consider lunch a yogurt that they eat as they're walking down the hallway. Or, even worse, I have taught with noneaters before. One teacher claimed to be too busy to eat, and she wanted to "watch her figure." One day after school, she appeared to be sleeping on her desk. In reality, she had fainted.

I cannot stress enough the importance of taking care of yourself. Please do not let this be you. To maintain energy and focus, you have to intake quality calories regularly. If you don't eat during the day, you will likely compensate with nonstop eating once you get home. Don't do that! Not only is it unhealthy, but also there is no badge of honor for starving yourself. That is self-neglect, which is the opposite message of this book. Focus on planning ahead for your food intake, choose healthy options, and don't ever skip a meal.

Tip #8: Keep Your Calm On

If you can get control over this area, you will be in great shape. We, as teachers, take on a tremendous role. Not only are we dealing with our own life and issues, but we are also absorbing those same things from our students. Therefore, it is totally natural to feel emotionally involved and connected to our students. But to that end, how do we manage the scope of emotions that may arise, and how do we maintain our own self-control in moments of profound frustration?

We cannot control circumstances, but we can control our reactions. This means that it is a wise use of our time to examine how we typically react when we are under pressure.

When something unexpected or disappointing happens, what is your reaction? Do you get mad? Snap at the kids? Gripe about it in the teachers' lounge?

Have you ever thought about what your students are learning from you in those moments?

They are watching us. They are learning, absorbing, and becoming what they see. We need to be a role model for our students. They are looking up to us for guidance and direction on how to handle life. I want to encourage you, above all things, to strive to represent yourself as the person you would like for them to be.

The biggest piece of advice I can offer you in this area is to not take things so seriously. I'm not saying don't care; just try to maintain the proper perspective. Sometimes the small things seem so big that we become delusional and overreact to them. But the reality is that we may just be making mountains out of molehills. If that is the case, we are unnecessarily inviting stress into our lives.

I remember when I learned this lesson. I was obsessing over school and the endless tasks ahead. I was staying late and bringing papers home to grade or lessons to write. It seemed that no matter what I did, no matter how much time I put in, I just couldn't get everything done. There was no "over" until the end of the school year. I think that is part of the reason it is common to count down the days until summer, because we will finally feel like we actually finished something.

When a tragedy struck my classroom (which you will read about in the next chapter), everything changed. I realized that everything I focused on didn't matter. All of my energy had been going toward the wrong things. I realized that curriculum and test scores were secondary to love and relationships. I realized that things that I thought were such a big deal were actually not important at all.

When I made that shift, everything changed. I made *them*, the students, as beautiful individual human beings, the center of my energy. When I did this, everything else effortlessly followed. My students were inspired from within to learn, and test scores elevated. I even won an award from the state for my proven ability to consistently increase student achievement.

The funny thing is, I was never focused on that! That became a side effect of looking at my students with love, respect, innocence, and potential.

I'd like to challenge you to discover for yourself what is really important, and let the small things go. I have come to realize that there aren't real emergencies at school. There are situations that need to be managed, but not emergencies. Don't let the small stuff ruin you.

Tip #9: Let Go of Perfect. (You Can't Fix Everything, and That's Okay!)

As difficult as it may seem, you simply cannot save everyone or fix every situation. You're not the parent. You're not a therapist. You're not a social worker, and you're not a savior. You're a teacher—a teacher with a heart and with passion, but you are one finite being who can't save the world, and that is okay.

There will be some challenging moments in your life and career when you realize that there is pain you cannot fix, there are problems you cannot solve, and there is injustice you cannot right. There will be times when you question if you could have done more, been better, seen the signs sooner, or just been a little more insightful or compassionate to prevent something that seemed avoidable.

As a teacher, you have to do your best to distinguish between the two. Then, you have to acknowledge that it is okay, you are not everyone's rescuer, and some issues are not yours to fix. In accepting this, you will find yourself better positioned to deal with those things you can address, and not bear the weight of the world on your shoulders.

Tip #10: Nurture Your Inner Hero

You're a hero surrounded by an industry of heroes, so sometimes it's difficult to realize just how special you are. You are a teacher, and you serve the next generation. You have a tremendous responsibility, and you rise to the occasion each and every day of your life.

Do whatever it takes to nurture your inner world so that you feel refreshed and fulfilled. Look within. What inspires you on the inside? Do you have faith in something greater than yourself? What is it that you can connect yourself to that makes you feel fulfilled? For example, right now I am writing this and looking out the window at the incredible

Rocky Mountains, feeling so peaceful. This is inspirational to me, and it changes something on the inside.

I also love having personal quiet time, reading, and being out in nature, taking it in, and enjoying it either through a heart-pumping activity or simply in rest. There is little I enjoy more than to breathe crisp, clean air, and think about all the things for which I am grateful. It doesn't take much for me. What is it for you?

Balance, Balance, Balance

Just imagine how great it would feel to be at a place where your time management skills are so strong that you can have a real life outside of the classroom. A life where you optimize every minute of the school day, and you leave with your head held high at the end of the day, proud of all that you gave and accomplished.

Remember that in order to be a healthy, well-rounded individual, you *must* have a life outside of the classroom. Do not make schoolwork your sole identity. You deserve to have a balanced life. Take time away from school each day and focus on yourself. In doing so, it will be much easier to avoid burnout and that feeling of being drained.

✓ Take time for yourself.

✓ Enjoy your weekends.

✓ Engage in hobbies that you used to enjoy.

✓ Connect to your spirit, mind, and body in a way that makes sense for you.

✓ Always stay balanced.

The more you take care of you, the better teacher you become, and the more lives you touch. It is not selfish. It is the most loving thing you can do for the students and the families you serve.

big picture management

Truth #7: You Will Have Life-Changing
Moments That Make It All Worth It

A teacher affects eternity; one can never tell
where their influence stops.
—Henry Adams

before we end our time together with this last, very important Truth, let's take a moment to look back at how we began. If you remember, we began this book in Truth #1 by discussing our "teaching bookends," focusing on *why* we decided to become a teacher, as well as the type of *legacy* we hope to leave. All of the Truths in between were designed to help you navigate and succeed at this wonderful journey called teaching. As you look back on your responses, are there any adjustments you would like to make to the answers you wrote? You may find that your hopes and dreams change as you grow, and that is normal and okay. I hope that throughout the instructional years, you hold on tight to your bookends, for they are the rocks that keep everything in place.

At the end of each school year, as you proudly place another "book" on your teaching bookshelf, I hope that you take a moment to browse through the pages in between and marvel at all of the life-changing moments that went by, because the journey in between the bookends is all about *life change*.

As teachers, we have the joy and honor of watching little lives change right before our eyes. For many of us, that is the reason we are able to show up day after day despite uncomfortable demands or difficult work conditions. For most teachers, nothing can replace that feeling of knowing that we can truly be difference makers. Even on those days that seem like they never end, we change lives. In the school years that surprise us with unimaginable obstacles and challenges, we change lives. As we feel beaten and bruised by politics, bureaucracy, constantly changing initiatives, overcrowded classrooms, and demands of accountability, we are changing lives.

As we overcome, overwork, feel underpaid and underappreciated, and wonder if this is all worth it, even then we change lives.

But what if I were to tell you that in committing your life to one of service, you could expect to experience moments that change *your* life as well? It's true. Through the giving and the caring, we change. It might occur slowly over time, or it might be something dramatic that suddenly happens. Every teacher's journey is different.

On our journey, we play many roles: we are the police officer, the detective, the doctor, and the nurse. We are the therapist, the firefighter, the lawyer, and the judge. And because of that, we have the privilege of seeing those life-changing moments unfold right before us.

When those life-changing moments happen to our students, we join in their change because that is the depth of our caring. We celebrate their accomplishments, and we absorb their pain and their sorrow when life sends them unthinkable circumstances. We become one with them, and then we realize these will be the moments that shape us.

When these moments occur, they remind us of what life is really all about. At least that's how it happened for me. My most life-changing moment in teaching was a day for which there was no training, no guidelines, and no preparation. It was the day that would ultimately become the day that changed me. In fact, I am not sure I would still be a teacher but for this day.

I was teetering on professional burnout, unsure if I could go on. But that fateful day reversed all the damage done and helped me to see life from a different perspective, one that allowed me to reconnect to teaching.

Do you remember my journal entries from the beginning of this book? This is how that story continues...

Dear Journal,

I am in my fifth year of teaching. It is hard. It is too much. I have no one to talk to about how I feel. I feel so ashamed. My personal life is in crisis, and I cannot deal with the stress of that on top of teaching. I desperately want to make a difference, but my students deserve better. I am sobbing as I write this, but I will be leaving my classroom in February right after the state tests. Me = failure. I will be moving back home, and I will try to figure my life out. I am desperate and I cannot stay afloat. I am so ashamed. Please help.

Kerry

.... ❦ ....

Dear Journal,

I have moved back home. I am substitute teaching during the day and waitressing at night. Even though I'm working all of the time, it actually feels less stressful than teaching. I miss the students, but at least there are no papers to grade all of the time. Maybe I will do this instead! Feeling better. Thank you.

Kerry

.... ❦ ....

Dear Journal,

Well, one problem with that plan. It is unpredictable. Some nights I am not needed, and there have been weeks where I haven't gotten any sub jobs. My student loans are piling up. Even if I did want to change careers at this point, I have no idea what I could do. And it would cost money to get trained in something new! Plus, I really miss the children. Right now I'm not making a difference in anyone's life, and that is depressing. I'm a waste. I don't want to live like this. I was born to teach. Please help me find a teaching job where I can make a difference.

Kerry

.... ❦ ....

Dear Journal,

Thank you! It took five hours of interviews and one demo lesson, but I have just secured a teaching job at a beautiful metro New York City school. I can't wait! I am going to start fresh! Thank you thank you thank you! When can I move in!?

Kerry

.... ❦ ....

And then, just weeks into the school year, my most life-changing moment occurred...

The morning of September 11, 2001, started like most days. I was teaching my third graders, and they were engaged, working hard on the day's math lesson. I was at the whiteboard explaining that in subtraction, sometimes we need to regroup. We need to "go next door and get 10 more." I was having fun with them, acting it out like a little skit and making a funny voice to help explain it. The kids giggled.

It was only 9:15 a.m. when the loudspeaker came on in my classroom, and the school secretary asked, "May we have Julia for dismissal, please?"

"Yes, ma'am, on her way," thinking it seemed early for one of my students to be picked up. But as Julia gathered her pink backpack and promptly left the room, the loudspeaker sounded again: "We need Nicki for dismissal." Nicki grabbed her things and left as well. Our math lesson continued and we all got actively back to work, although something inside of me felt weird. I couldn't put my finger on it. Even the students thought it was strange to have two dismissals so early.

Suddenly, at my classroom door was our team leader and fellow teacher from the classroom next door. The look on her face screamed something was wrong. I told my students to continue working quietly while I stepped out into the hallway to find out what was going on.

"Are you okay?" I asked, my heart racing because I knew the answer.

"No," she said. "New York City is in trouble. The Twin Towers have been hit by airplanes..." I remember very little after that moment.

"…parents are lined up out front wanting their kids … has a son who works in the towers … parents work …"

I could only hear fragments of her sentences and was unable to fully understand the meaning of what she said. "The City," as it is called, was a simple commuter train ride in. I was frozen in shock, and then my mind began to race.

Which students have parents who work in the city?

Who do I know who works in the city?

What teachers in this school have sons and husbands who commute in?

What is happening!?

She continued, "We are doing an immediate dismissal. Do not tell the students what is happening. Use the words 'national incident.'" And then she quickly walked away to inform the next classroom.

I had to take a breath of air in that moment. I was on the verge of panicking and completely shutting down. *I can't do this! How do I handle this?* I somehow gathered myself and re-entered the classroom.

In that millisecond, I looked at the delicate faces of my students and was consumed with the terrible scenario unfolding just a few miles away. In that moment, I felt as if I were on the cusp of robbing these children of their innocence. Their world would be forever changed, and nothing would be the same. I couldn't even consider that one of their mothers or fathers lost their lives in that tragedy. I knew those sweet, pure, blameless children had just lost their opportunity to grow up in a safe and protected world.

I felt an overflow of emotions:

This is wrong!

I am not strong enough for this!

I don't understand what is happening!

The little girl in me wanted to cry and be held.

Thankfully, somehow pushing out through the fear, the teacher in me rose higher than the scared little girl. I realized I was the only adult in the room, and had to handle the situation to the best of my ability. I had to figure out how to explain to the children that school was suddenly over for the day, without alarming them or scaring them. I knew I had to change the expression on my face, because no doubt, it displayed shock.

I immediately relaxed my face to one of pleasant calm and slowly walked toward my desk, pretending that nothing was wrong. As I approached, I told the students to continue with their assignment, that I was proud of them for working so well, and that I would be right with them.

Those 45 seconds were the longest of my teaching life. I had to think about how to handle the situation. I knew that I had the power to make this okay or further the anxiety they would almost certainly feel. I knew these kids would remember this day forever. They were going to remember how their teacher handled this moment. I cannot even describe the weight, the burden of responsibility I was feeling. In the forefront of my mind was, *I know they need a strong leader right now, but who am I? I am a plain old teacher, only in my sixth year. What am I supposed to do? I am clueless. I know they need me, but ... what?*

Finally, I took a deep breath and began. I do not recall my exact words, but I know they were something like:

"Everything is okay. I don't want you to be scared, but we are going to be going home right now." Twenty-three pairs of wide eyes stared at me. Frozen silence at every desk.

"Your parents are coming to get you. Don't worry; everything is okay. Your parents will explain to you what is going on. It is a *national incident*."

I used those exact words, even though they were likely as confusing to them as they were to me. We packed up our belongings and gathered on the carpet as a family.

The questions were aplenty.

"No, there is no homework, sweetie. I want you to just be with your family and enjoy a night of no homework."

"Yes, we will have school tomorrow."

"No, you don't have to worry about the science projects."

"Yes, we will reschedule the buddy reading session."

"No, you do not have homework" (again).

"Yes, your sister is going home as well" (ouch).

All the while, students were being dismissed one at a time over the loudspeaker. One after the next, after the next. We could hear the speakers from the classroom next door, and it was just as quick and often as in our classroom.

Their minds were racing (so was mine!), and I did everything I could to keep peace and calm order. They were my priority. I didn't matter. All I could think was, *how can I make them comfortable?*

I decided that the best thing I could do to get everyone's mind off the obvious was to do what any teacher knows works like magic: read to them.

I grabbed our lighthearted chapter book and began to read to them in a loving, nurturing way. We were immersed in the story line, and some of the kids were even upset because they had to go home before the story ended. I told them not to worry; we would reread it.

And off they went.

As I watched each student leave, I wondered: Is it her? Is it him? Are they about to hear news that will forever change their life?

A New Way of Thinking

And on that single day, my perspective on everything changed. All of the problems and stress in my life were exchanged for perspective. It was in that moment when I realized how important our role as teachers is and how delicate and precious life itself can be. That day brought me clarity I'd never experienced before or even knew existed.

That moment renewed my entire classroom existence. It suddenly became completely clear to me what was important and what wasn't. Lesson planning, test scores, data, busy-ness, all gone. In its place: love, family, relationships, gratitude, and proper perspective.

This catastrophic time, including the terrible weeks and months that followed, was a paradigm shift. That renewed perspective is the reason for my joy as I interact with my innocent students every day, and I feel honored to be entrusted to look after them. I learned to not let the small things ruin me, because isn't it all small things, after all? I do not allow myself to overthink things anymore, and I no longer look down at the ground and see dirt and garbage and problems all around me.

Instead, I learned to look *up*, and have gratitude. I have learned to make genuine eye contact with my students and *smile* at them. I learned to try to find the beauty and wonder everywhere, instead of focusing on the difficulties of everyday life. Because the truth is that most things are not all that difficult. I now sort out the truly important things in life from those that aren't all that important.

September 11, 2001, offered me a tremendous amount of insight and a life-changing moment. The losses were clearly not worth the insight, but we are no better off if we do not learn from any tragedy, even one as significant as that one. I hope you'll never have a moment like this in teaching or otherwise, but if you do, moments like this remind us why we teach.

As teachers, we are given the responsibility to protect the innocent, elevate the sad, and do all we can to teach our young students to handle life, even when it seems unbelievably unmanageable. That day gave me no choice but to shed my personal pain and grief, and prevent my students from feeling the same. They needed me to be strong for them, and while I wasn't perfect, I tried my best. You will, too.

If you ever find yourself in a situation like this, do not be afraid. You can do it. You can rise to the occasion. You can and you will be the leader that they need in those moments. When and if moments like this happen, the reasons you became a teacher suddenly show up in a mighty, strong way. You don't have to plan for it; it just organically occurs. And you don't need to feel strong on the inside in those moments. It's okay if you don't. What is important is that you consciously present yourself as a calm leader for them, even if you fake it.

Every day, let the small things go, and focus on the things that *really* matter. You are worthy of having joy in your daily life, and so are the multitudes of lives that you touch every day in this most noble profession. Hold on tight to those special reasons that drew you to teaching, and know that the life-changing moments that happen along the way make it all worth it.

I promise.

love the journey;
stay encouraged

I know that your time is valuable, and I cannot thank you enough for your willingness to spend time reading this book. I hope that it was helpful, and I hope this is just the beginning of our relationship together.

I would love to hear from you with your feedback, thoughts, stories, concerns, or questions.

Please feel free to email me at teachersfieldguide@kerryhemms.com or contact me via my website at kerryhemms.com

Even in the tough times, keep your bookends close at heart, reach toward your legacy, and always remember what was mentioned in the beginning:

- 💗 **You matter**. You are a hero. Your decision to join this profession of heart-centered individuals makes you extraordinary.
- 💗 **Your happiness in this profession matters.** You deserve to love your life as a teacher. You deserve to have the tools and strategies you need to make an impact without losing your life and mind in the process. I hope you found them here.
- 💗 **You are not alone.** I've been there. I get it, and I am committed to making sure you feel supported and encouraged in the process. Please let me know how I can help you.

You can do this!

www.kerryhemms.com

about the author

Kerry Hemms, MEd, is an award-winning, United States Senate recognized Master Teacher with over 20 years of experience in the educational field. She has directly instructed over 3,500 students and worked to influence over 10,000 students in her numerous leadership roles. Sadly, over the course of her career, Hemms has watched great teachers leave the profession because of discouragement, frustration, and stress. When this happens, they leave behind empty classrooms, confused students, and lost dreams. With a vision for all students to be led by teachers who know they matter and feel supported, Hemms is driven by her mission to help strengthen and encourage the teaching force by bringing awareness and solutions to the global teacher recruitment and retention crisis.

Morgan James
Speakers Group

www.TheMorganJamesSpeakersGroup.com

We connect Morgan James published
authors with live and online events
and audiences whom will benefit
from their expertise.